A REASON WHY TO
ASK WHY

To Answer Questions of Why
Leads to Personal Freedom

Mark A. Murray

A Reason Why to Ask Why
To Answer Questions of Why Leads to Personal Freedom
Copyright © 2018 by Mark A. Murray

Scripture quotations marked KJV are from the Holy Bible, King James Version (Authorized Version). First published in 1611. Quoted from the KJV Classic Reference Bible, Copyright © 1983 by The Zondervan Corporation.

Library of Congress Control Number: 2018955261
ISBN-13:   Paperback: 978-1-64398-267-0
            PDF: 978-1-64398-268-7
            ePub: 978-1-64398-269-4
            Kindle: 978-1-64398-270-0
            Hardcover: 978-1-64398-271-7

Printed in the United States of America

LitFire
PUBLISHING

LitFire LLC
1-800-511-9787
www.litfirepublishing.com
order@litfirepublishing.com

Contents

Introduction

I am Mark "the Welder" A. Murray, better known as Mark the Welder. I have been a welder for almost forty years. I call welding my God-given talent due to the fact that welding came easy for me. It is like I have always had a certain understanding or knowledge of how to weld most anything.

The unique thing about something that is or has been welded is, it joins or bonds two separate pieces on a molecular level. Unlike gluing two pieces together, it actually melts two pieces into one solid piece. This is very similar to whenever we cut ourselves. After a healing period of time, the wound grows back together and becomes one with itself. Though there is usually a scar that remains, the place where the cut was, is as strong after healing as it was before it was cut.

Perhaps you are thinking to yourself this is all well and good; however, what does it have to do with this book? Well, even though I have been very blessed with a trade that affords me with a better-than-average standard of living, I am coming to one of those stages in life where it is time to prepare for the future.

I am fifty-seven years of age, and since welding is something that requires a fair amount of physical strength and good vision, I have probably another ten to fifteen good years of productivity in the welding field. I have also pretty much lived a life of reckless abandon, as do so many construction-type workers.

I come from what I term as "the working poor" background and have no retirement or inheritance to count or fall back on. What I do have is a wealth of life experience and knowledge on how to enjoy and live life in troubled times. I have come to a life experience that is full of love and understanding that is pretty much free from judgment, jealousy, and all those fear-based hang-ups we all face in life.

I no longer fear death; however, the best part is, I no longer fear life. I have broken free of many addictions, religious problems, and beliefs that confuse most of the populous—past, present, and future. This is not to say I don't have my ups and downs in life, like everybody does. I just move toward finding solutions to my problems much faster these days.

I no longer delve in self-pity or carry blame. I am not afraid to love or receive love. I know who I am, what I need versus what I want. I know the difference between what a dream is versus what a fantasy is. Let's just say that I am as mentally stable and comfortable with myself as I have ever been in life. Even more so than most of the counselors I have seen.

The important thing here is that I now know *why* I have this beautiful state of mind; therefore, I know how I have achieved this wonderful state of mind. It hasn't been an easy journey, and it took a lot of reading and asking myself and others—professional psychiatrists, priests, chaplains, psychics, mediums, and plain ol' people—those uncomfortable questions on "why you think like you do." I joined Bible studies, was baptized Catholic, and have finally come up with a sensible answer to who and what God is to me.

I have no problem with the atheist and completely understand why they believe the way they do. Though I am a religious person, I do not support any one religion over another and find them all very interesting. However, I am most interested in the power any belief has on the way we look at our personal world. The different ways we think, believe, and apply faith have everything to do with what we achieve and don't achieve.

Perhaps you can see that I find myself in an interesting situation here. I have this wealth of self-help information that I have spent many years acquiring. I know that a lot of what I say, and the way I say it seems to really help the people that are around me. I find that even the new people I meet in life have messages that help me as much as my messages help them.

I have also found that I have a rather powerful urge to write. I find that I spend several hours a week writing. Though my welding business pays my bills and keeps me busy during the day, I more often than not wake up in the middle of the night, usually between the hours 1:00 a.m.–3:00 a.m., with lots of ideas and thoughts that feel important for me to write down. Most of the time, these writings have a certain person whom I have either just met or ran into for a focus. The focus usually has to do with something this person is struggling with in life.

Pretty much always, when I pass the information along to the person, they thank me and say it was pretty much exactly what they needed to hear. This usually makes us both smile and results in more energy for use during the day. So this all has led me to writing the first of several books I am going to write.

Though I may lack the elegant verbiage that a road scholar uses, my target audience really doesn't care to have to go to the dictionary so often. I feel in my heart that my simple philosophy can help most anyone, despite their educational background. However, the ones who will benefit the most, I am afraid, are not usually the reading type. Therefore, I am going to keep my first books short and easy to read. I just need to come up with good titles so that I will attract those who will benefit the most from what I write. It seems to me if I can create new readers, then the whole literary world will benefit.

The next challenge I am facing is the publishing phase. Actually, the part that I enjoy the most is the writing. I write everything by hand, so even though my spelling is getting better and will continue to improve through time, just like my penmanship has come a long way, what I really would like is a person, or persons, to whom I can hand my writings and who can do editing also. Perhaps you can help me find the correct people I need to assist me in my new journey to becoming a writer.

Though the couple of people I do know who have been published say that the Amazon thing pays better, is cheaper, and is easier. I think it more important to get my writings into the hands of those who will benefit the most from them. Therefore, it only makes sense to me to find a publisher who knows and understands the distribution process. The way I see it, it is going to take me some time to develop my writing skills and learn what the book world really is all about.

I have plans to write several more self-help books on things like forgiveness, addiction, fear and anger, and common topics like that. I also have some ideas on fiction I want to attempt. There are also some things on the art of welding I want to do.

If they are done well enough and I get the right publishing and editing people, the money thing will take care of itself. I am just trying to supplement my income and develop a skill that I truly enjoy so that when I feel the physical abuse of construction and welding ten years from now, I have something to do.

How many retired welders do you know? I only know of one crippled one. To be frank, the thought of trying to survive on social security, to me, is anything but gratifying. I know panhandlers who make more money than social security pays. However, since I have experienced a life of homelessness for a short period of time, I know and understand how it happens and why one doesn't have to settle for that way of life.

There are a few who actually choose that way of life. They find comfort in the simplicity of it. I, myself, don't! To each their own, and who am I to judge? I much rather enjoy the power of the universe that we all have access to that comes in the form of love and life energy that is as infinite as the stars on a warm, clear summer night. This is a part of what God is to me.

To be able and willing to harness and use the power that comes in the form of the written word, to me, can only be defined as divine. I can only believe that you know and understand the power of the word better than I.

So, before I turn this simple letter of introduction into a book, please take a little time and read my first attempt at getting published. *A Reason Why to Ask Why* seemed to be a good one with which to test the waters. "One can't know the temperature of the water without at least putting in one foot," as the saying goes.

Thank you for your time, and I look forward to hearing some constructive criticism.

Chapter 1

Why Thought Is
the Mother of Intention

As I sit here on this very snowy Mother's Day, I can't help but marvel at all the variety of life outside my cabin windows. Hundreds of blackbirds, chickadees, magpies, finches, sparrows, and even hummingbirds dart through the flakes of wet, heavy spring snow. The snow has piled up a soggy two-foot blanket on the ground. It will nourish all the plant life that has been waiting for such an event to explode into blossoming growth.

The warm light of the giant ball of bountiful energy we know as the sun will show through the perfect filter of our atmosphere in the next few days. The warm, shining rays will melt this snow quickly into another perfect dimension which we know as soil or dirt. Dirt contains all the building blocks required for plant life. The plants, in turn, produce a new form of food and nourishment for insects and animals. The insects and animals enjoy a consciousness of life that is filled with curiosity and a certain amount of intelligence, which I refer to as instinct. These natural instincts tell these insects and small animals they are different from other species and how to recognize their own.

Have you ever wondered how species recognize their own kind? If not, then why not ask yourself? It is not like they have a mirror to know what they themselves look like.

How does a bee know it is not a fly or a wasp and vice versa? How does a mouse know it is different from a mole, or a small pack rat, or a chipmunk? I'll bet they don't even care what they themselves look like. I wonder if they were to see themselves in a mirror if they would recognize the reflection as themselves or even if they would consider it to be anything other than a shiny piece of glass.

The truth of the matter is, there is an intelligence in all species that tells them what food is, what is a predator, when to breed and with whom, how to care for offspring and for how long, what to fear and when. In short, there is an intelligence which informs all species of all things necessary to survive.

Even the little games baby critters play is the perfect practice to gain the skills they need for survival. The young observe the mother or adults doing whatever it takes to gather food for the energy required for life, whether it be hunting prey or gathering seeds and roots. They watch, learn, and play their little survival games of life. The harder they play, the stronger and better they get at the survival game. All this activity of playing hard is part of the law of nature which leads to stronger species of all types.

As human children, we are pretty much products of our environment. If we have a stable, loving environment, we generally turn out stable and loving. A baby in the womb has an idea of what its life will be like in the last stages of pregnancy through what Mom experiences.

During infancy, the little one learns all the rules that apply to its world from those who are around it. This process of domestication is not unlike the way we teach dogs and cats through punishment and reward. Our society is also governed this way through punishment and reward. This sounds simple because it is. It's when you expose them to all the different religions that confuses things.

As children, we mock and practice what the adults do to prepare for life. We do this through playing with pretty much anybody who's willing to play with us, young or old. This natural instinct to play is with us until we die. Anything fun we like to do, anything that's scary, or triggers the natural instinct of fear—we don't like to do. This is all well and good if all the people practiced what they preach all the time. Even then, there are so many different beliefs in the world a child can, at best, be very confused. Any action that happens out of confusion can only lead to more confusion. So we are left on our own to figure out the confusion.

Good judgment comes from experience; experience comes from bad judgment. Man is constantly attempting to control the world around him by making laws which he believes will control the actions of the people. I call these *man's laws*; and they have nothing to do with the laws of nature, which include the law of gravity, magnetism, and things which keep order in the universe.

Everything I state in this book comes from my personal experience. Though I try and back everything I state with scientific facts, there are some things us humans haven't even come close to figuring out the truth of yet.

I have a theory on the whole "parent trap" situation. It appears our definitions of a man and a woman are cloudy at best, so my definition goes like this: the difference between a man and a boy is, a boy has mating on his mind first and a man has survival on his mind first. A girl has the thought of a man as providing security where a woman has the mothering instinct on her mind. Therefore, the law of nature makes a boy of around eighteen *horny*, for lack of a better term.

This is due to the fact that a boy around the age of eighteen is in his prime, as far as the body's ability to spread healthy genes for the strength of the species is concerned. A woman is usually eleven years ahead in maturity, to assist the probability of survival of the species. However, our society's and old society's beliefs have looked at the female as not being naturally more mature and the male thinking he is superior. This has really put a damper on the evolution of us humans.

The egotistical attitude of the males, which comes from the natural law of the stronger male makes for a stronger species, has interfered with our growth as a species. If you ever watch the strength and determination any female animal has when it comes to protecting her young, you will see even the alpha male of a breed back down. If not for the Virgin Mary, Jesus would not have stood a chance. Her natural instinct as a mature young lady is the only reason Jesus survived. Perhaps this maturity naturally stops her from creating conflict with the alpha male.

The best that can happen is, life where all involved grow for the good of the species despite age difference. This makes the most sense to me as to why people tend to misunderstand the whole "finding a mate" thing. I also believe the reason time seems to fly as we get older has a scientific explanation, thanks to Edison. The faster an object goes, like the speed of light slows down time, means to me when you're young, you're always in a hurry to get to the next life experience so it appears to take forever. But the older you get, the more you are trying to slow down time so the faster it goes.

This natural law falls under the same category of all laws of nature. Just like the law of gravity, these laws of nature are absolute. They are the "what is" in the game of life. They have nothing to do with man's law—right or wrong, good or bad. They are just what is. They are part of the divine truth that is guaranteed in the game of life.

These laws of nature are the same throughout the entire universe and are perfect. Without these laws of nature, all that *is* could not exist. This includes the physical dimensions as well as the nonphysical dimensions. Though science and people such as Einstein talk of many dimensions, I am referring to the two which make sense to me—the physical one being things you can see through your eyes and feel through touch and the nonphysical you see with your mind's eye and feel with emotion. The nonphysical is where your thoughts and dreams live.

What I am referring to when I talk about your mind's eye is all you envision when dreaming or thinking. Perhaps you can remember a time you were looking at something with your physical eyes but can't remember what you saw because you were thinking and envisioning something else that was on your mind. I am sure you have seen someone staring off into space, daydreaming about being somewhere else. We can choose with which eye to focus. Many times, I will close my physical eyes as to allow myself to concentrate on what I am trying to see in my mind's eyes.

Life has a natural energy which creates movement and flows in and through everything in existence. This life energy is made up of electrons, protons, and neutrons. Different combinations of these particles make up the physical dimension of the universe. Everything that is vibrates with a form of life energy. The divine source that drives this energy, which creates all that is, to me, is what God is. To me, the god particle is the electron. The force which tells all these tiny particles to clump together in all the various ways to form all that is in existence must be divine in all senses of the word. Whatever sparked the big bang was rather divine, don't you think?

No matter what one believes the truth to be, the fact that we exist and everything around us exists cannot be denied. No matter how you try to explain it doesn't really matter because it is what it is. The nature or truth of everything is forever morphing and changing, that is for sure; just as sure as there is no doubt we are constantly changing, and growing, and alive at this moment. As a matter of fact, everything that is matter at this moment is moving and living, and this is a fact. It is all about the energy. Though there are different types of energy, I will focus on physical and nonphysical energy.

Physical or kinetic energy is required to move something that has mass. Nonphysical energy is thought which create emotions. There is electrical energy created by magnetism. Electrical energy is the same energy our body uses. The brain contains billions of nerve cells arranged in patterns that coordinate thought, movement, behavior, and sensation. It is these nerves that transmit electrical signals. This is the clinical definition. Your reading these words, whether you understand them or not, is a movement of energy in two different dimensions.

The physical dimension in which you are looking at and holding this book requires energy. This physical dimension contains all you see through your eyes and feel with your touch. The other dimension is where your thoughts live and exist with everything else in your mind. Your mind uses the nonphysical energy you know exists because it creates the sensation of feelings you experience inside—all that you cannot physically see or touch. This is the nonphysical dimension you experience through your mind's eye.

This dimension contains all the other dimensions which live outside your physical world. Everything else in the universe you cannot see or touch lives in the nonphysical world or dimension. What we refer to as consciousness lives in the nonphysical dimension. All the questions we ask ourselves is nonphysical energy.

The reason why I believe we have a need for a nonphysical dimension is to have a place that is infinite, unaffected, and unrestricted by time and space. Once nonphysical energy is created, it is also eternal. As soon as you take your thought energy and turn it into words and write those words down on paper, this same thought energy becomes a physical form and is transferred to every being who hears or reads and understands it. It doesn't matter how many times it is copied or transferred; the energy lives on. Every time someone tells a story to another person, the energy lives on. Even though the thought energy is eternal, it requires physical energy to create and transfer it.

The action of talking or the action of writing requires your physical energy to make it happen. The printing press requires physical energy to make the copies. Any machine that plugs in, comes alive when the electrical energy can flow through the On switch to the rest of the acting parts. Electricity is physical energy that can be seen and heard. Thunder and lightning are a good example.

We eat food for energy, and that food we ate required energy for it to grow. Plants receive minerals from water and the soil, along with energy from the sun, which stimulates growth. All life is a sharing of energy from the physical to the nonphysical and back again.

One creates the other; however, the other doesn't survive without the flow of energy back. This flow of energy is what life is, and everything this energy touches experiences life. This, to me, explains the reason we would need multiple dimensions. It also helps me to understand that because there is a nonphysical dimension where thoughts and ideas live, there must be a dimension where spirit or soul energy can also live.

I also believe the Great Creator is as simple as being energy in both the physical and nonphysical forms. God is energy, and energy is God. Therefore, God flows through and around all existence—always has and always will. The Creator lives through our creation; therefore, we live through God's creation. How perfect is that?

This is perfect creation through the harmony or flow of energy through everything. We are God only because God flows through us in the form of energy. God lives through us living from God. Is this not a good definition of the word *divine*?

The word *god* is very powerful and creates much emotional energy in humans everywhere in the world. I believe we, as individuals, need to examine the emotion inside us that is created with this word. My intention is not to make you believe one way or another but to help you understand why you believe what you believe.

I'm afraid the religions of the world totally miss the boat on motherhood; for if not for Mom, we wouldn't be here today. If we ignore what we do to Mother Earth, she will soon ignore us. However, in thousands of years, she will heal and bring back life with perfect balance. Sounds like a Bible story we have where the leading role is confused to me. Perhaps this is what is meant by the Bible story where Jesus returns and defeats Satan's armies and then there is a thousand years of peace, as prophesized.

If you become lost, what is it you do? Hopefully, you just stop and look around and get your bearings or retrace your steps back to where you did know where you were going. Don't be afraid to ask someone for guidance. Just be aware of the natural law of attraction. If you keep doing what you are doing, you are going to keep getting what you are getting.

Directions that come from someone else who is lost will surely lead you to more people who are lost. It's hard to see where you are going when you are following a confused crowd. Perhaps this is why one finds themselves in a riot when that was not what they intended. If you are lost in a crowd, the most reliable person for truth should be the mother with children.

Therefore, it seems to me the chicken had to come first because without Mom to incubate the egg and nurture the little one along, you can't have a hatchling. The mind is where thought, or the "seed," is born; and only through or with this intent does it come to fruition.

Chapter 2

A Simple Lesson on Energy

Perhaps you don't feel like you need to understand energy any more than you already do. Without energy, there is no life. If you understand energy, you can get much more out of life. If you know how energy flows, you can learn to flow with life. If you had more energy, would you not do more things in life? How many times have you watched young ones playing while thinking to yourself, *I wish I had some of their energy*? We all wake up with a certain amount of energy to use during the day and waste most of it on things we don't even realize. It's all about the energy.

The simplest way for me to help you understand what energy is would be to describe what and how electrical energy works. Though electricity is only one form of energy, it is something we humans have come to depend on—way too much, in my opinion. Though electricity brings me many different forms of enjoyment and is absolutely required in my trade in the art of welding, I sometimes practice in my mind what my plan of survival would be without it. This usually only happens during power outages, imagine that! How often we fail to appreciate something until it's gone.

The basic laws which govern electricity are absolute, just like the law of gravity is absolute. The cool thing about electricity is, it relates to life and society in many ways. To have a basic understanding of one helps explain the other.

The word *electricity* itself ends with the word *city*. There have been government studies that have applied the laws of how electricity works in circuit boards in comparison to how society reacts to the flow of political power, and you can pretty much predict how the flow of humanity will react to the application of that political power. I read about this in *Behold a Pale Horse* by Milton William Cooper.

Electricity is made up of electrons, volts, and amps. Electricity is created by the movement of positive-charged particles which build up to a point where they discharge to ground or a negative. A generator or power source, such as a battery, discharge the electricity which then travels on or through what is termed a conductor.

Wires and metal bars are the most common conductors. Water is also a conductor. Electricity, once created always flows toward the path of least resistance to ground. The earth we stand on is negatively charged, so it is the ultimate ground.

There are two basic types of electricity. Direct current, or DC, and alternating current, which is called AC. Our houses use AC, and our cars use DC. Most things in the home run on single-phase 110-volt AC or 220-volt AC power. Big motors and industry run three-phase AC power mostly.

There are many interesting trinities, or factors of three, which exist in life. AC, DC positive, and DC negative are one trinity that governs the natural law of electricity. The compound H_2O is a basic essential need for life. Made of two hydrogen atoms and one oxygen, water is yet another factor of three, or interesting trinity, that is a fact necessary for life. Electric power or energy flows through water; therefore, water is considered a conductor. There is a constant flow of electricity, termed *stray electricity*, which flows underground throughout our planet. This is what corrodes metal pipes and tanks buried underground.

We often hear about trinities, or the factor of three, in many things, including religion. There is something about three that stabilizes. Three legs on a table won't wobble. Three-phase electric power is best for industrial machines that need to be powerful and able to turn or rotate in forward and reverse. The energy that religious groups get from talking about God, the Son, and the Holy Spirit is very palpable when you sit among then in church. If God and the Holy Spirit are one and the same, are we not shy a factor for a trinity?

To me, spirit energy is the important part here. Electrical energy needs three basic things: a conductor to flow on or through a source, a positive and a negative, and a ground. Just like spirit energy would need a source, God perhaps is a conductor or a body to flow through—like human, animal, or any life-form—and a place to flow to, like ground or a planet.

In our bodies, the brain is the source and our nerves are the conductors which control the muscles. Nerves relay what we see, hear, and feel back to the brain. Our brain uses actual pulses of electricity to move our muscles. This is how a Taser incapacitates bodies. The electrical charge overrides the electrical signals from the brain. A Taser works off just a 9-volt battery. Electricity flows through water rather well, and since the human body is made up of mostly water, electric current flows through us easily. But when it does, it overloads our body's natural flow of energy.

A factor for electric energy to flow requires a conductor for the energy to flow in, on, or through. All metals are conductors; however, some metals, like gold or copper, have the least resistance, so the energy flows more freely. The simplest explanation for the way electricity flows is to compare it to water from a garden hose. Water comes out of the valve and runs through the hose to the sprinkler, out onto the ground. Electrical energy comes from the power plant that runs through the wires seeking negative or a ground.

Another factor for electric current to flow requires both a positive (the source) and a negative (the grounding point). This process or flow of electric current is called *direct current*, or DC negative. DC current can be made to flow from negative to positive also. This is DC positive. AC—or *alternating current*, which is what our households use—is where the electric current bounces back and forth between positive and negative.

DC can be stored in a battery, and all batteries have a positive pole and a negative pole. AC requires a generator or alternator continuously generating a current flow. Though AC current cannot be stored in a battery, it can be converted or transformed into DC power or current, which can be stored in batteries. DC can be converted or transformed into AC; however, it requires several large DC batteries and a transformer to achieve a little AC current. Another cool thing about electricity is gravity has very little, if any, effect on it flowing straight up.

Though there is a never-ending supply of energy which comes from the sun, wind, and the flow of water in rivers, the ever-so-powerful energy companies find it more profitable to burn coal or natural gas to turn the generators that create electricity. Perhaps we should ask ourselves why we should allow giant corporations to pollute and profit from something of which there is a clean, never-ending supply. It almost seems money has become more important than the preservation of life.

Perhaps when you think about electricity and the light bulb, the name *Edison* or *Nikola Tesla* comes to mind. Tesla understood electricity better than our best scientists today. We still use the same electric motor design he developed. He is why we have AC power in our homes today. He was working on a wireless electrical system that would have given the whole globe free power.

When JP Morgan heard about this, he cut off the funding he was providing Tesla. In Colorado Springs, Tesla was lighting up light bulbs with no wires and no batteries by sticking them in the ground a mile away from the power source. The best the universities of today have done is only a couple of feet.

Tesla was infatuated with the power of the numbers three, six, and nine. When he died in his hotel room on the third floor in room 33, or some multiple of three, the US government seized all his paperwork for his designs of death rays, lasers, and things the military has developed into the superweapons we have today. He and Einstein worked together on the Philadelphia Experiment for the military. He had ideas on antigravity devices and electric cars which would run on the natural stray electricity which flows throughout the whole planet and also from Tesla coils in strategic places.

Do you ever question where these humans we label geniuses get their knowledge? Most of them all say the same thing—all humans have access to all the knowledge of the universe. Most say it comes to them in their sleep.

The point I'm trying to make here is, all the thoughts we have are made of nonphysical energy. We know they are energy because of the emotion we feel in our bodies. We can choose what to think about—whether it stimulates bad feelings or good feelings—it is our free will. This would also create the possibilities of us drawing information from the nonphysical dimension where our thought energy resides, the place which contains all information.

I am not trying to discredit the genius's academic achievements. However, we are all made up of the same things and have the same-sized brains. Some have just learned how to use more of it than others. A lot of times, near-death experiences will come with visions of the future, especially if electric shock is the cause.

The way electricity is made or generated is by taking two magnets and running them past each other without touching. If you have ever played with magnets, you find there is a natural law of attraction in one direction along with the law of nature that repels in the opposite direction. This magnetic law is like all other natural laws. Just like the law of gravity, they are what is. Though invisible, there is no doubt they exist.

I believe this magnetism is created naturally through the spinning of the earth around the molten metal and rock in the core of the earth. Since we have the North and the South Poles, which resemble the positive and negative of a battery, the magnetic energy has direction, which is why a compass will always point north. This magnetic field is also what protects our planet from all space is throwing at us. This natural magnetism, I believe, is what keeps the planet spinning as well. Though science can prove many things in life there is a whole lot of speculation mistaken for fact. One has to learn to take all information with a grain of salt; for lack of a better term.

Our history should be rewritten every time facts disprove old beliefs. We have access to all the knowledge in the universe, but if you don't even believe in a nonphysical place or dimension, you won't even try to access it.

All the energy this natural process creates is physical energy because it requires a physical act of something to create it. Therefore, it is affected by space and time.

When a thunderstorm builds up and comes rumbling through, the physical action of the clouds and wind create a friction between the particles in the positively charged sky and the negatively charged ground. When the buildup of the positive particles reaches a perfect balance, *boom*, lightning connects with the ground. This physical action of energy being created is best described as static electricity or sometimes as an act of God.

When you see God as pure energy, to me it proves the power of God is always present and happening. If a tornado forms due to the perfect balance of warm air rising into cold air above, one sees the destructive power created. This wind energy destroys anything man doesn't build strong enough to withstand it. When this act of God happens, even though man has the knowledge to avoid it, he calls it bad. But it is just what it is. Any house built in Tornado Alley is a form of Russian roulette. If you jump in front of a bus, do you blame the bus for running you over?

Since time and space have a part to play in this physical creation of energy, it is just a matter of time before it will happen again and again. Since God is all energy and all energy is alive—just like thought energy is alive in the form of knowledge or the act of knowing—God is always present in the form of energy. To me, when I see God as nothing more than pure energy, it creates something I, myself, can believe in. It seems to me the harder science tries to prove an absence of God, the more they prove the need for a higher power or thing that best describes as

God. The all-powerful, good god, in my mind, would fix things if he is what religion says he is. God doesn't have to punish man because man punishes himself in the name of God.

Humans waste so much personal energy trying to convince themselves that other people who appear to have faith must be smarter and better informed rather than taking the time to look to themselves for the answers to life's questions. The only person we can truly know is ourselves. This is why we need to become self-aware in order to use energy in the form of thought wisely, as to learn what they truly enjoy in life. If you waste all your energy on hate and anger, you will experience a whole lot of hate and anger toward you. It is your free will to use your energy to your liking or not.

Energy can only flow through a conductor with a connection. Since thought knowledge is nonphysical energy living in a nonphysical dimension, it isn't governed by space or time. The only way we can connect to all universal knowledge is through a nonphysical connection in the mind. We just haven't learned how to use that part of our brain. A lot of us don't even believe the world is older than a few thousand years yet take the time to see ourselves as a nonphysical spirit driving this physical body we call ourselves.

The fact of the matter is, all energy flows because of and through the positive and negative. It is the law, not man's law, but the law of nature or God's law. Whatever name you choose to give it doesn't really matter because it is what it needs to be. All energy is born and governed by the positive and the negative, whether physical or nonphysical. It is a result of the natural magnetism generated by the planet or the movement of electrons. This awareness, to me, allows for the belief of why thoughts good or bad, positive or negative, can attract more of the same. Free will gives us the choice to think and believe what we want to agree with or not.

Positive and negative is how all energy is born, and one cannot exist without the other. This includes all thought energy, which is eternal and responds, and attracts, and repels through the positive and the negative. Once one becomes aware that all energy is governed by the natural law of attraction due to the positive and the negative, they then can use free will to flow naturally with the law.

Chapter 3

On Knowledge and Wisdom

Now that we have learned a small amount of knowledge about the way energy moves and flows always to the path of least resistance, let us move on to discussing resistance, which is another part of the law that governs energy.

When electric power meets resistance, it creates heat and light. This is how light bulbs work. The resistance of the small wire in the light bulb is where the heat and light come from. The resistance from the small wire in the light bulb heats up, and that is what creates the light. To me, thought energy is comparable in the way that when we think about something we don't agree with, we will meet the thought with resistance or fear, which creates heat in the form of anger, which eventually leads, hopefully, to enlightenment.

When one is enlightened, they come to realize thought is only energy and possibly not true. I try to limit the power or energy I focus on thoughts, which create fear or anger. I will often question myself as to why am I feeling this anger or fear. Is it based on an assumption or a truth? Can I even know if it's a truth? Do I need more information?

Is it even my thought, or does it come from someone or somewhere else? Have you ever had a thought come into your mind that you don't know where it came from?

Allow me to refresh. Our thought energy lives in the nonphysical dimension. Therefore, we see these thoughts through the mind's eye and feel with emotion. Electric energy is conducted and controlled by generators and wires. Thought energy is created in the mind, which is converted to physical energy by the brain, which controls and conducts the physical energy to and from the nerves.

The brain is the physical, and the mind is the nonphysical. The nerves carry signals of feeling to the brain and also the pulses of energy back to the muscles for movement. The brain's job is to control and create the movement of physical and nonphysical energy between the different dimensions. The thought the mind thinks is the nonphysical energy. The brain then turns the nonphysical energy into physical energy, which moves the body parts or stimulates emotion.

The thoughts we have are made up of words or the language we have come to know through our life. Thoughts also contain visuals, audios, and all things we experience through our senses.

Knowledge then, to me, is nonphysical and best described as alleged knowing. Knowledge is what thought energy is made of and is the only thing the mind can use in the art of creation. The alleged part of knowledge is due to the fact most of what we think we know isn't true. The truth is alive and always changing. What is true today might not be true tomorrow—another good reason for living in the moment.

Knowledge is made up of everything we have ever learned, seen, or heard. Knowledge contains everything that has been taught or sought throughout the whole universe from the beginning. Knowledge is how we know everything we see or think we see exists. Perhaps you have heard Descartes's famous statement "I think, therefore I am." Knowledge is how the nonphysical thought energy influences the physical world. Knowledge contains all that is and all that can be. It contains all that might be and all that isn't. Knowledge is what allows the physical and the nonphysical to intermix so the brain and the mind can cocreate, with physical and nonphysical energy. Everything we believe or don't believe, all that is stored in our mind in the form of memories is knowledge.

From the nonphysical powerful energy of knowledge, we create everything we know to be true and false. Knowledge is all the data we are exposed to. The brain and the mind can be compared to a computer and cyberspace. The brain is the computer and the mind is the cyberspace.

The cyberspace a computer uses is limited to the world's servers and many rooms full of hard drives collecting and storing data. This is science fact. Ask a scientist or the medical world where the mind is located, and there is no way they can pinpoint it. All we can do is observe the physical things happening electronically in the brain.

We can electronically stimulate parts of the brain and help depression and some memory loss. Other short-circuits which lead to seizures, however—there is no way to physically prove the existence of the mind. We know we have one only because we all possess the ability to think. Thought, of course, can be impaired by brain damage or chemicals; however, you can't deny we have a thing we call the mind.

The brain, just like the computer, needs power to work. The computer you plug in gets power from electric energy, and the brain gets its energy from food. The brain creates actual electric pulses and uses this to function. When we buy a new computer, it comes with an operating system which enables it to remember and communicate with other computers. Once this computer goes online, it understands and is susceptible to all the information fed to it. All the information that is fed to it comes from all the humans and other computers who know and understand the operating system.

Humans and animals are also born with a natural operating system. Science calls it DNA. As infants in the womb, we begin storing information or memories in the form of visuals and audios—the sound of our mother's voice and her surroundings. I think we must feel and experience our mothers' anxieties and stress while in the later stages of pregnancy.

As soon as we learn language, we have nonphysical data or knowledge we retain in memory. The more language we understand, the more knowledge we retain. I hope you know by now that any information you access or feed your computer online never goes away. Even if you destroy your computer, the information is still out there. Therefore, data or knowledge is eternal nonphysical energy, just like thought energy. It never goes away. You cannot unthink anything. You can, however, avoid a thought by not giving it focus or physical energy.

If your computer gets a virus, it gets slow and jams or quits working altogether, just like if we get a virus it affects us in the same way. A computer virus is nothing but data or information which confuses the computer program. A physical virus that we get in the animal world is a living set of cells which stay alive by fooling our cells into replicating into virus cells. When the cells of our body figures this out, it firewalls the virus cells.

Most all the vaccines we get are made from the same virus cells, except in small doses and are combined with other cells that have information our body recognizes to be a threat. Then our body builds a firewall to protect us from that particular virus. A lot times, this lasts the rest of our physical lives. Such is the case with smallpox or measles. A virus is very much a living cell that is doing everything it can to survive. It can, in time, outsmart the antibodies produced in response to a vaccine by mutating.

As a people, we are also affected by nonphysical viruses that come in the form of thought. These thoughts consist of things that we may believe about ourselves. Most of the time, these false thoughts come from fear or any one of the labels we have for thoughts that create emotion.

We often will take things other people say to us to heart, even when we should know they are not true. We so often judge ourselves based on others false beliefs. Many of these false beliefs have been passed down for many generations. We need to pay attention and learn to question ourselves and our thoughts to become self-aware. With self-awareness, one learns to firewall this negative thought energy and/ or false beliefs.

When a computer becomes infected by information or data that we call a virus, we introduce information or remove data or knowledge, which eliminates the confusion, so the computer operates or thinks more smoothly and faster. Though we as humans would label a virus bad, a computer only sees this information as conflicting. Once someone who understands the computer language goes in and corrects the confusion, which resolves the conflict, then the computer works fine.

The point I am trying to make here is, information or knowledge in and of itself isn't bad or good, unless it stimulates feelings in us we label good or bad. A computer doesn't have feelings; therefore, it doesn't look at information as true or false, good or bad. It's just ones and zeros. As soon as someone who is well practiced in computer knowledge comes into the picture, they go into the mind of the computer, eliminate the confusion, and then it computes properly and smoothly.

When a human develops a mental illness, it is much like a computer virus. We as humans need to understand, mental illness is usually the result of something traumatic or abusive happening to the person. If a young person is sexually abused for multiple years, they normally act out with violence and anger or even become sexually abusive themselves.

We so often punish or try to treat the acting out, instead of finding out what happened to cause the acting out. Perhaps if we ask them what happened to them, the answer to why they are acting out will be obvious. Then we can focus on their confusion of why things happen, and let them know they are not alone, and create a pathway to healing instead of a road to hell in prison. Young minds are all brilliant until we give them viruses we believe to be true. We all have some thought virus.

There are those who tend to use some mental diagnoses or illnesses to their advantage by allowing the diagnosis to be an excuse for undesirable actions. Is not the reason we know this only proof we have done this ourselves at some time in life? Who hasn't called in sick when they weren't that bad?

One of the problems with mental pain is the injury is nonphysical, so it is hard to see. Many will self-medicate with drugs and alcohol to numb the mental pain. Some will self-mutilate in order to create pain they can physically see. Cutting oneself to override mental pain is only temporary at best. If this describes you, please understand you have many options to find help; and I assure you, you are one of many who is living with the same problems and fears, past and present. What doesn't kill you makes you stronger. Something good always comes out of something bad, though it may take time to see it. It's the law of nature to maintain balance in life. Without positive and negative energy, life can't flow.

The important thing here is, if this isn't you, then it's not your problem. It is more important for you to recognize how often you lie to yourself and why you lie to yourself more than it is to prove someone else is lying. One can be empathetic without expending the energy to feel bad.

You can't expect a person who lies to themselves to be honest with anyone else. We are all human and designed to make mistakes. I heard somewhere, "A wise man learns from his mistakes; a genius learns from somebody else's mistakes." Our denial system is a place where we lie to ourselves to keep us from suicide.

This brings us to the intelligence part. I define *intelligence* as an interalliance we have with ourselves and energy—both physical and nonphysical—to understand knowledge. Once we become aware of what knowledge truly is, then I say we start to have self-awareness. We become aware that knowledge is nonphysical energy that only uses up our physical energy if we let it.

Most of the time the thoughts to which we are giving attention have nothing to do with what we want or need. Just like a computer which uses memory to store knowledge, we have memory that is there to help us create. We either create with intention, attention, or by default. If knowledge had physical mass, it wouldn't work or fit in the physical dimension, hence the need for another dimension, which is eternal and not restricted by time and space.

If one would put all the books and writings on this planet in a pile, it would make a mountain of substantial size. Though we have all this knowledge written in books, we wouldn't waste our time trying to read them all.

Nonphysical thought energy or knowledge, though eternal, is always old. Since all thought is based on past experience and what is in memory, there is no such thing as a new thought. We may have new ideas; however, as soon as we think, it is always in comparison to the past. We tend to think, *I could have, should have,* or *would have.* Hindsight is twenty-twenty, however. He who looks backwards runs into things. He who looks forward learns to avoid these conflicting things. It is all about the energy and creation.

We are all trying to create a situation for ourselves that is secure and enjoyable. As simple as this sounds, most people are always wanting more. Perhaps this is due to the fact we spend more energy and thought on all the reasons why we can't have what we want. There are many who don't even know what they want, or by the time they figure out what they want, they tell themselves it is too late to achieve it.

The definition of *insanity* is doing the same thing over and over expecting a different result, as the saying goes. We are all guilty of insane thinking at some time. I believe it is a glitch in our DNA. Whatever it is, we can use it to our advantage.

Everything has two ways you can see it. It has to be this way, or life would stall or stagnate. Life is life, only because there is a positive and a negative—a yin and a yang. You can't have one without the other. It is through intelligence one discovers what one wants and why they want it. Then we need to focus our thoughts on how we can achieve it. Once you can envision a way to achieve what you want, then you can focus your intention in the moment and on the action it will take to achieve it.

Really, the true intelligent way to use thought is to remember how to get home, what has worked before, and how to communicate honestly and clearly. The thing about thinking is, it requires physical energy to think, which requires "food for thought"; and since we only have so much physical energy for the day, we waste a lot of energy thinking instead of doing. Actions speak louder than words, though sometimes the best action is nonaction. Without action, nothing happens.

Intelligence is the interalliance we have with ourselves using thoughts or feelings. We must pay attention to what we honestly feel and know. All the knowledge in the world does not make a person intelligent. An intelligent person uses their knowledge to cocreate a harmonious world with others, which naturally brings joy to all parties involved. It happens all the time.

Though one experiences ups and downs in life, the positives and negatives are a must, for you cannot have one without the other. "Nothing but sunshine makes for a desert, which is also full of life," another adage goes. The intelligent use of knowledge to cocreate enjoyable experience is part of the art of wisdom. Good judgment comes from experience, while experience comes from bad judgment. The knowing that, with free will, we can control what we think about is intelligence. Intelligent thinking leads to learning anything we might want to learn. Once we learn to think with our interalliance, which contains all that we feel and do, then we think for ourselves. This leads to self-awareness.

It is only with self-awareness could we create or cocreate the life we choose. Once we learn to use our thinking intelligently, we control knowledge. When you control knowledge, then you know you can achieve whatever you put your mind to. You then practice what it takes to achieve what you want. If what you practice doesn't conflict with the life that is around you, then you have wisdom.

The art of wisdom comes from learning both good and bad practices. If the action you are doing and gaining from is bad or comes at a cost to others or your environment, then it will be short-lived at best. The negative energy others you harm produces may take a while to catch up with you, but because it is only energy, it will. It's the law of nature.

Why create conflict when conflict keeps you from creating a life of happiness and joy? Why not learn to create the life you want without conflict? Life is much easier and takes less physical energy without conflict.

A wise person always has a look of comfort in their eyes due to the fact they are well practiced in dealing with conflict. A wise person is content most of the time because of their self-awareness. They know how to say no and when to say no. They know what they want and how to get it without conflict.

A wise person knows how to control knowledge and what feelings are for. A wise person has found the path of least resistance in their life. A wise person has answered the *why* questions and is working on the *how to*. A wise person understands that there is a high power of nature's laws and chooses to work with the law instead of against the law. A wise person can look at this higher power being best defined as God. A wise person can work with most anyone to cocreate in a way that helps all parties involved.

I am a person who has clinical depression and fights anxiety. However, I am no longer on medication for it. I would never suggest stopping your medication without consulting both doctor and pharmacist; however, learn all you can about why the medication works for you. Perhaps a natural alternative will work better. A wise person knows the ups and downs in life are necessary, and to give in to or accept a diagnosis doesn't allow room for the power we possess to self-heal. Through self-awareness, we can develop our abilities to help heal others—not to mention ourselves—with the energy nature provides.

To me, this also gives credibility to how Jesus, the biblical person, may have miraculously healed those they say he healed. Perhaps you are now experiencing the energy or power thought creates after reading the last statement about Jesus. It is all in what you choose to believe or put faith in.

The whole concept of God is so controversial, it is the source of many wars both past and present. Since I am not out to make you believe one way or another, I will save some of my theories for other books. My reasoning mind believes science should prove why something godlike, or a force which steers the energy life, is needed. So for now, I will just label the energy that is life *god*, because you cannot deny the energy that derives from the word itself and the power and control it has on thoughts of so many, believers and nonbelievers alike.

To me, the answer to the question *why* needs to make sense in the way it fits scientifically and historically with the motive. All action starts with a motive whether it's good, bad, or natural law. If the word or concept of god creates a need to argue or prove one way or another of God's existence, then you really need to question yourself on why you believe what you believe. If the word *god* creates a sense of fear, you need to figure out why for yourself. Only you can answer this question for yourself.

To live in fear requires a lot of energy. Fear comes from confusion, and any action made from confusion only creates more confusion. So if you are seeking God through other people's opinions, then you will experience much confusion. If you seek something, you will always find something. However, most of the time, people settle for someone else's beliefs. This is why only you can answer the question of *god* for yourself. You will know by how it feels.

As humans, we tend to interpret knowledge in the ways we want it to be. As eyewitnesses, we are horrible at best, due to the fact we are constantly in dream mode and our brain is so good at creating a whole picture. Even the blind sees a picture in their minds as to motivate or get around. Therefore, the Bible, to me, is a fine storybook and a pretty good history book. However, since it was put together by someone who battled against Christians and knew the power of fear as a motivator, they chose which eyewitness writings were included.

I am skeptical about all religious books and the power they have to control those who are looking for something to have faith in, other than themselves. The one book I have faith in and recommend on a daily basis is *The Four Agreements* by Don Miguel Ruiz and is very much my inspiration for writing this book. I have seen this book change people's lives for the better more than any other book. It is an easy-to-understand and simple set of principles to follow.

The Four Agreements: A Guide to Personal Freedom consists of these four things: (1) be impeccable with your word, (2) don't take anything personal, (3) never make assumptions, and (4) do the best you can. As easy as they sound, it takes lots of practice and devotion to live by these agreements. However, the energy and power one receives to protect themselves and live in a world of negatively confused, mentally unstable people can only be realized by experience.

It seems the people who have the most to benefit from this knowledge are the least likely to find it on their own and the most likely to reject it before giving it a chance. This is because of fear or other beliefs they may fail to realize they even have. Hence the subtitle of my book, *To Answer Questions of Why Leads to Personal Freedom.*

The feeling of curiosity may have killed more than the cat on one hand, but curiosity has led to all that science has showed us, and it is where the knowledge we have about ourselves will come from. Curiosity is where the questions of *why* begin; and with the knowledge we acquire, we can—with wisdom, experience, and by what we feel—make intelligent decisions.

It's time to rewrite the history books to include all the things we, along with religion, have gotten wrong. It is no wonder why the Ten Commandments have turned into many various religions and beliefs, due to the fact we are very complicated in the way we think and believe. Science is constantly rewriting their books in order to correct the knowledge they contain. Religion needs to do the same thing because to err is human, but to not correct false knowledge will only continue to create confusion. This is anything but intelligent thinking.

Chapter 4

Some Truths about Feeling

Have you ever questioned yourself about feelings, why you are feeling what you are feeling? Have you ever noticed how much physical energy feelings require? I very much like the feelings that increase my energy level.

Have you ever taken pleasure in feeling bad? Some people do. A lot of people, however, take pleasure in other people feeling worse than they themselves do, though they would not admit to it. We have a whole big variety of words and labels to describe feelings such as *anxious, scared, happy, sad, jealous, mad, bad, glad, hungry, full, hot, cold, comfortable, pain,* and the list goes on. The thoughts we have are very influential over the feelings we feel.

We have physical feelings such as things we touch, and we have nonphysical feelings like worry and anxiety. Nonphysical feelings also create physical feelings. Though I don't like to label thought energy as good or bad, it helps me think about feelings as either good or bad. If you pay attention to your feelings, you find feeling good gives you energy while feeling bad uses your energy. Though fear gives you energy by releasing adrenaline in the body, you feel drained after you come down from the adrenaline rush.

What if life were as simple as doing what feels good and you will have all the energy you need to achieve all that you desire? Sounds pretty much like heaven to me. Believe it or not, life is that simple! This "if it feels good, do it" attitude or strategy to living life obviously needs to follow moral guidelines.

If what you gain is someone else's loss, you pay for it in the loss of energy eventually. The problem is, we don't believe life can be simple. We have convinced ourselves life is nothing but suffering and punishment until we die. The haves in life are worried the have-nots are going to take what the haves have. Do you ever question why we never seem to have enough?

My favorite saying in life is, "If it weren't for self-inflicted wounds, we would have no problems!" I coined this phrase many years ago, and people have mixed reactions to it. Even if you are in the right place at the wrong time, your choices led you there. The only exception here would be the child who has no choice in what a parent does. The biggest hurdle we have in life is what we believe.

If you are afraid of feeling bad, then you will feel bad—a lot. Part of the reason for this has to do with the natural law of attraction. The same law which makes magnets attract causes thought energy to attract more of the same. It takes physical energy to hold magnets apart, just like it takes physical energy to think.

It is our free will that decides on thinking and feeling in a positive way. However, if you turn a magnet around, it will repel the other. Let it go and it will return to the original position and stick together. Are you following my logic here? You have to focus energy on positive thought, or the law of nature acts out of default to line up the negatives.

You have to realize that other people who are in a negative mind-set will put you in a negative state of mind if you don't pay attention to thought.

We have the ability to observe our thoughts without reacting to them. It takes less energy to just watch our thoughts come and go than it does to allow ourselves to feel the emotion they may stimulate. With practice, you will notice—long as you don't focus on a thought—you won't feel the thought. We also don't have to feel bad to be empathetic.

Feelings have so much power involved, we are not sure how to handle them. The thing is, the feelings are only the result of thought energy. Have you ever noticed how the pain of an injury doesn't hurt until you think about it? I believe anesthesia works because it stops conscious thought. This is for major surgeries. The use of drugs to numb a specific area are a type of nerve block. Usually, you don't feel pain until you look at the injury either through your physical eyes or the nonphysical mind's eye. It is thought that creates the feeling, so change the thought and you change the feeling.

As a volunteer fireman, I also acquired an emergency medical technician certification. As an EMT basic, I was required to work in the local hospital. Between there and all the ambulance calls I went on and was part of, I saw a lot of injuries, car accidents, a few shootings, and too many suicides. I was always amazed at people who complained about the injury they could see and not even realize a more severe injury they couldn't see.

This is physical pain that comes from physical injuries. People who have a mental illness experience nonphysical mental pain—meaning, you can't physically touch or see it. When the fear of living exceeds the fear of dying, then suicide can be the result. Dying is easy; it's living that's the hard part.

The interalliance that emotion and feeling has with the physical body to control knowledge is what I see as intelligence. The reason we feel bad is mostly caused by what we believe. The same holds true with feeling good. The only difference is to feel good, which gives us energy, and requires the action of holding positive thoughts against the negative. Otherwise, the laws of nature line up the negative thoughts, which drain the energy we need to act or think positively.

If you think about it, it just has to be this way—follow the law, make it work for you, and gain energy. Do nothing, and the default takes over and takes your life energy. When you do something nice for someone else, everyone who witnesses the event gets a little positive boost of joy and energy. However, this works best if the acting party has nothing but good intentions.

If a party acts to help someone but does it at the cost of others, most of the time, you will find the ones who pay the price (or the ones who lose emotional energy) are in a negative state of thinking. "When it rains, it pours," as the proverb goes. Anytime you find yourself feeling like you are better than anyone else, the universe tends to produce a lesson in humility. Some call it karma. Others call it luck. Those who have an open mind will always see the good things, even when bad things happen.

Feelings, bad or good, are our internal guidance system for life. They are much more dependable than a GPS. Feelings cannot be denied. They can be changed if you answer the question of *why am I feeling what I'm feeling?* The only reason you feel what you feel is because you think what you think. The only reason you think what you think is because of what you believe to be true.

Stick to the only laws of truth, the laws of nature. The laws that govern energy naturally govern people in the same way. The positive and negative work the same in the physical and nonphysical dimensions.

Psychiatry says that sociopaths don't have feelings. I tend to believe they are just wired differently. They get their energy from the negative. They have no remorse because it is not in their DNA. You can't tell me they don't feel good and get pleasure from their destructive paths they walk.

The reason a sociopath can walk into a room of three hundred people and pick out the easiest victim is because they sense the negative energy the victim radiates by default. Victims are victims because they, more often than not, don't pay attention to their gut feelings. They tend to be warm, good-hearted people who wouldn't harm a fly. They are usually the people who stand out because they try hard not to stand out. There is nothing wrong with being shy, however, beware of the other shy-acting person trying to make small talk with you.

Sociopaths are almost always practicing on how to entice a victim. They are usually predators of opportunity more so than looking for a specific person. This holds more to psychopaths who get their biggest rush out of torturing and killing people and animals alike. They are very good at using statements like "I sure hope my ride shows up" to lure you into conversation. If you engage with something like "I have my own ride," you are probably in for a strange conversation where this person has a lot in common with you and most always is the victim of circumstance.

They say one in twenty-five people have sociopathic tendencies. Therefore, the odds are pretty good you will fall into one of their little games. A couple of important things here are not what the correct label may be for this type of person, as much as it is to recognize situations where people like this may take advantage of you.

I, myself, find motive the best place to start when assessing any given situation I may find myself in. What is the motivation to why another person is associating with me? Are they just being friendly, or do they want something from me? If this person is giving me more information than is normal, then what is the reason why? If this person is a stranger to my world, too much information should be a red flag.

People will flood another person with too much information for other reasons which have nothing to do with being a sociopath. It is still a red flag. There are many who use drama to manipulate others for various reasons.

A sociopathic person is usually very sure of themselves, especially in knowing how to control another person, by creating a sense of fear in the other person. A sociopath derives a lot of energy out of the fear another shows when they are being controlled. Therefore, this makes the sociopath feel good.

Though all sociopaths don't turn into serial killers, they do plenty of damage in other ways. The most important thing to realize here is, the gut feeling we have in any situation needs to be realized. The source of fear we experience ever so often is always the first sign of something about to happen. One would be troubled to find a more powerful motivator than fear. "We have nothing to fear but fear itself"—Franklin D. Roosevelt gets the credit for this statement; however, I doubt he was the first to use it.

If you fall victim to a person with sociopathic tendencies or anyone who tries to get a rise out of you, the best reaction is no reaction. You have nothing to gain out of self-blame for falling victim to someone's game of manipulation. Some are pretty good at it. Just try to remember the gut feelings which may have preceded it.

One could make fear the topic of a whole book, and there are many books on fear. I myself like to think of fear as a gift that just keeps on giving. What I mean by this falls along the lines of my belief where the universe will present us with all those scenarios we fear the most.

The answer to why this happens can be attributed to many things. Perhaps just thinking about something you're afraid of gives it all the power it needs to come to fruition. Maybe you feel a need to overcome a certain fear, so you create a situation in order to do so. Perhaps you don't think you even care about something you are afraid of, so you try to avoid it. The important thing is the action or reaction fear creates.

Please don't misunderstand me here. We are all people of many colors. I, myself, am 25 percent Native American and find myself wishing it was more. The truth is, we are all just people of the human race.

There have been many cases in history where groups of people have enslaved other groups of people or tried to eliminate certain people because of different beliefs. It is still happening today. This is despite the majority knowing there is something wrong with this behavior. The only thing to change this struggle for power is to realize the only world we have control over is the one in our own mind. I am the only person I need to control, not to mention I am the only person I can control.

We get back what we put out, and as long as we give the past energy—because of fear and anger—the more power the past has, to happen again in the present. Though we need to remember this, I believe we need to let the pain of the things of the past that weren't right die as not to bring it into the present. The job of the angel of death is to let the old painful things die, so there is room for the new healthy things to live.

Perhaps this is what the Bible meant by the resurrection. Maybe all the old ideology was supposed to die with Jesus; but we, only being human, misunderstood the parable. Everything has two ways of being looked at; even a mirrored image is opposite.

Please understand that this philosophy of mine is geared toward adults. A child that falls victim to adults has circumstances that don't really allow an escape from the abuse. The laws of nature can be thought of as cruel at times. This is part of what I mean by life requires both negative and positive.

Most animals in captivity that sense overpopulation or overcrowding will go to eating their young. Nature is always in the process of maintaining balance. The fact that the young and the weak fall prey to predators makes for a stronger species and preserves the strength of the herd or species makes perfect sense to me.

The young colored man who falls victim to the gun of an officer usually is the result of fear of both people. The young man fears the officer because of the past history. Many people are still angry about what happened in the past and fear that it is going to be history repeating itself. As long as we delve in the past, it will continue to have power in the present.

The officer carries the "it's either us or them" fear. The officer has learned that usually, when someone shows signs of fear, it tends to mean that person has guilt and therefore is afraid of getting caught. The officer is taught that if the officer is too slow on the draw, he or she will be killed. Perhaps this is why so many shots are usually let go.

An officer fears anyone who gets away is likely to kill or abuse others, including their own family. The problem isn't racism as much as it is the problem that comes from the fear of what *has* happened or what *can* happen. It is hard to focus on what is happening if one is focusing too much on the past or the future. Violence to stop violence is just more violence. As long as people fear the officer, the officer will fear people. It doesn't help that as humans, we know someone who is afraid of us are usually easier to control.

The way I deal with the thought of people who abuse other people is with faith. I have faith that everybody gets what they have coming to them. It's just a matter of time. It is not my place to judge, convict, and punish others for actions I deem wrong. A lot of people put faith in believing that God and/or Christ is coming to fix everything in the future. This is all well and good. However, as soon as people try to force beliefs on others, this action will almost always result in conflict and violence. Do you ever wonder why we believe someone or something else will save us from ourselves? Is it not due to the fact religion has preached this for a couple thousand years?

I have faith in eternal life as being something that just is. To me, my belief that my spirit is nonphysical energy which just resides in this physical body as long as the body is alive makes perfect sense to me. I have seen and heard enough evidence that proves to me that a spirit or ghost leaves the physical body when we die. If God is what energy is, then spirit energy would be made up of and in the same likeness as God, would it not?

But then I can also make sense out of extraterrestrials coming to this planet thousands of years ago and genetically altering or modifying a species or ape with their own genes and DNA. This would then make us hybrids that would easily be controlled through knowledge or thought energy. We could all be a somewhat evolved slave race that aliens used for gathering and mining gold for some advanced technology. After they got what was easy, they moved on or are just observing us from afar to see what we evolve into. It is not really that farfetched to me. However, it kind of screws with the religious beliefs, or does it? My God lives through me here and now and something watching from above is alien.

I believe all the answers are in the DNA that science calls "junk DNA." If you don't understand what the facts are, how can you determine the facts that are important? It's like having the input shaft out of a transmission. By itself, it just looks like a funny piece of steel. However, a machine or car could start up, run, rev up, and pretty much do everything but move without the input shaft. To the untrained eye, however, the shaft just looks like a piece of junk.

To me, DNA is kind of the same thing. We just haven't figured out what all the parts mean. I am pretty sure the truth will come out, probably not in my lifetime. Nonetheless, we have come a long way since we stopped burning witches at the stake. I know that my life has improved immensely since I have started focusing my thought energy to learning solutions to my world. I have learned that it is more important to help one another and focus my thought energy on what doesn't interfere with nature's law or man's law.

If you don't focus your thought energy on creating your positive world, then all the negative things in your life are your own fault. If you don't focus your energy on creating anything and you are just trying to cruise along through life, then you, by default, attract negative energy. It doesn't matter what one thinks is right or wrong—it is what it is.

Until you focus your thought energy, which in turn attracts like energy in a positive or negative form, in both the physical and nonphysical dimensions by the law of attraction, if you don't give direction to your creating, then the default is negative creation.

Since most people do what feels good and that, to me, is a positive energy direction, then in order to balance the energy flow naturally, the default must be negative. But just in case everyone figures out this flow of positive and negative, the ones who are wired backward maintain the negative flow of energy for creation. It is not right or wrong—it just has to be.

If you don't feel good, it is your own fault. Only you can create a life that feels good to you. Pay attention to your feelings and live in the moment with intention, and by the law of attraction—the law of nature—you get what you intend.

As soon as you give energy to thought, positive or negative, you begin to attract more of that kind of energy. If you don't know what you want, your feelings will tell you what you want. Ignore your feelings and get what you expect. Why not expect a better life to happen? You do have to be honest with yourself. You are in charge of your reality. Even free will can come at a cost.

Chapter 5

Becoming Aware of What We Believe

To believe or not to believe is an important question. Do you ever wonder why some people are easier to believe than not? Perhaps we know how easy life would be if everyone was honest. Why would that make life easier? It wouldn't stop people from misunderstanding.

In this day of instant information on a global basis, we now have a new term called *fake news*. NEWS ALERT! All information humans pass along, whether fact or fiction, contains both fact and exaggeration; therefore, some fiction has fact.

If you break down the word *believe* you see three other words also live in this one word—*be*, *lie*, and *live*. Belief is a loaded word in my book. It can *be* or will *be*. It could *be* or should *be*, might *be*, might not *be*. "To *be* or not to *be*" is a question answered more completely when you add the questions *why* or *why not*. If you find the answer to *why* or *why not*, then you can move to the action of how.

In the middle of the word be-lie-ve is the word *lie*—can be a *lie* or might be a *lie*, would I *lie*, or should I *lie*. Most of the time we lie because we fear the truth. We will lie to ourselves because we don't like the truth. How can we expect someone to be honest with us when they are not even honest with themselves? If you find it easy to lie to others, it is because you are well practiced from lying to yourself. If you don't see the truth in this statement, you may lack self-awareness. It is more important for you to recognize how often you yourself lie than it is to prove someone else is lying. To live your own truth is what sets you free to live life on your terms.

This is why I believe the third word in believe is the word *live*. No matter how you arrange the letters, you cannot spell the word *truth*. This doesn't mean that truth isn't alive or doesn't live in our beliefs. However, we should be very careful and expect some of our beliefs to "be lies."

Since our human nature requires the need for a wonderful thing we call the denial system (not to be mistaken for a river that flows backward in Egypt), we have the denial system to protect us from sensory overload. We go into shock when we experience severe physical trauma, and when we receive severe mental trauma, we have the denial system to allow us more time to process that information which may scare us to death. I think our denial system has been altered by Hollywood and video games, not to mention any unnatural ways we stimulate the adrenaline rush.

The reason we "re-lie" on our beliefs so much is due to the fact that the feeling of safety we receive from them seems true. Have you ever wondered why we seek the truth so desperately? I know, for me, truth feels safe and it seems to give me energy. To discover the truth in something always is accompanied with the sensation I equate to the feeling of freedom.

Feel is another word you can spell using the letters that live in the word *belief*. However, *safe* or *safety* cannot be spelled. Therefore, what we believe really requires a second look. Not that this little game of wordplay has any significance really, perhaps just a coincidence. The power that resides in all language in the form of words is truly magical.

Back to why we put so much faith in what we believe. I truly believe it is due to the fact that words are an accumulation of nothing but nonphysical bits of thought energy, or knowledge. Perhaps every time a word is stated, it holds more energy. This would explain why the word *god* creates so much emotional energy. If energy accumulates in words we use to communicate, several words in the English language carry lots of power. All letters contain the energy necessary to explain and understand all creation from here to infinity and beyond! It is very dangerous when people have faith in things that are not true.

My brother, Patrick, asked me the question "What is bigger than infinity plus infinity?" My brain and all thought stalled. Then he told me of a situation when he asked a third grade class the same question. Their response was instantly stated as "To infinity and beyond!" This Buzz Lightyear line is from the movie *Toy Story*.

The answer makes so much sense, I couldn't help but laugh. The truth of the matter is, a nice, young third grade mind is fresh and not polluted with all the crazy beliefs an older person carries. Therefore, a reasonable answer came quickly. The third grade mind is all about the action of playing life. Third graders are in a constant state of looking forward and asking why. These brilliant young minds are sponges for any and all the knowledge fed to them, good or bad.

Third grade was a rough year for me if my memory serves me correctly. The personality of a person in the third grade is getting into high gear. A personality is almost all made up of what beliefs a person has. The belief system is the main source of energy or nonphysical power we get from our knowledge to create our life. The belief system is where nonphysical energy turns into physical or the kinetic energy that creates action. The stronger the belief, the stronger the action. As soon as a human being is positively sure about something, it will protect its belief to the death. We label this *faith*.

Religion is a powerful example of this. Politics is another powerful example. Most all the wars ever fought are over these beliefs. All war is fought because of some kind of belief. Some fight just because they believe they can win. *Win* is another powerful three-letter word just like *god*.

Have you ever paid attention to how some words stimulate feelings? It is like hearing a name of someone who you believe or feel has wronged you. How about the word *fear*? Now that is a word many books have been written about. Please don't think I am against religion or politics and all that dogma. Though religion does help some live a life that is morally desirable, it makes sense for a government of the people for the people, as so many are only thinking of themselves.

Let's just say my life has become much more enjoyable since I have come to an understanding about the world of addiction. Maybe we are addicted to the thought that tells us we must suffer in order to achieve. Some of this belief must come from the Bible story of the crucifixion. Perhaps since Jesus suffered and died for our sins, one feels a need to suffer also.

Beliefs are the sole source of all the negative stuff that creates our personal hell in life. Beliefs also carry the power to motivate oneself to achieve pretty much anything in life they so desire. Answer the questions of why you want something, and if it doesn't go against the greater good, the universe will help you—if you believe it can.

As soon as I realized that all these beliefs, in short, are just what creates the flow of energy from the nonphysical to the physical, I use my free will to create a plentiful, satisfying life using the laws of nature. I figure, just in case there is no life after death and this is all there is, I want to enjoy it for all it is worth. Does that not make sense to the alternative?

I find the more energy I focus on enjoying life, the more energy I have to create my own little heaven here on earth. I believe it's part of our free will, whether we experience heaven or hell in life. It makes more sense to me, in order to teach us, God would know that it would have to happen in the *now*; or we can't understand it.

I have come to the realization, all the conflict in my life has come from what I believe. If what I believe is at all possibly not true, then why not focus my energy on the truth of today because I can create my own truth the way I want it. One needs to realize, you get back what you put out. The golden rule of "do unto others as you want them to do unto you" doesn't mean you need to get even or punish others when they don't follow the rule. I am sure you have heard the statement "The truth will set you free." I am free from judgment because I have a better understanding of the conflict the belief system causes. Therefore, I am free from the judgment others have toward me. Better yet, I am free to believe in what makes sense to me.

All this newfound freedom makes me so happy, I wrote this book to help anyone who reads it. If what you believe leads you to an argument that cannot be proven one way or another or is based on what others have said or wrote, then it has the possibility of being a misunderstanding. Why try to force any kind of belief on someone? How do you respond to anyone who forces their beliefs on you?

It is not important to me whether or not you believe this. What is important is, if this simple philosophy works to help me avoid the conflict and confusion which leads to war, then it may help others in the same way. All wars start as a small personal conflict that grows in power to a group of people who agree an aggressive action is required to prove a belief. Take away the confusion on what a belief is, then I expect less war will be the new belief.

The power and chaos which comes from what we term *crowd mentality* isn't very often a good thing. Just observe what happens in a city who has won a world championship of some kind. The amount of energy these people release from being happy usually leaves cars turned over and people hurt. I believe it proves my point of feeling good gives you energy.

Chapter 6

On Language and the Power of the Word

In the beginning was the word,
and the word was with God,
and the word was God. (John 1:1, KJV)

"In the beginning was the word, and the word was with God, and the word was God"—how does this statement feel to you?

Does the word *god* cause a reaction? Perhaps only the first line makes sense. Does the word *god* scare you? If so, why? Perhaps you have been told your whole life the wrath of God is to be feared. Perhaps you are just sure Darwinism makes enough sense to you that it is probable everything evolved from a single cell. If so, what created the cell?

Does the word *atheist* cause a reaction in you? Does the word *atheist* cause you to draw a picture of a red-horned devil with a barbed tail? Why? Why not? Does the word *god* bring you a calming sensation and cause you to draw a picture, in your mind, of a nice old wise man with his son Jesus by his side? Perhaps just a cross with the Lord Jesus comes to mind. What does the word *sin* mean to you?

What you believe is not important to me. What is important to me is, you become aware of the words which stimulate emotional feelings inside—not only physical feelings but images you see in your mind, visions or pictures you see through your mind's eye. Why is this important? Because 90 percent of our suffering comes from our unconscious thoughts and visions which occur in the mind.

I view words as a form of magic we use to create. We can use words to create a wonderful, joyous, heavenly world, which to me is positive. We can also create the opposite, which I will term *hell*, or *negative*. The best part is, we truly have the choice.

The way to choose a positive way of life requires action. I don't know anyone who really chooses a negative life. Why would you? This proves to me, negativity is the default since they are both necessary for life energy to flow. You can't have one without the other; it is just nature's law. There are those who act out negatively. However, they may be punishing themselves or are just angry at the world they feel has let them down or betrayed them.

I found that I really have to pay attention to the way my mind uses language and focus it on the positive. When I look at language, I am not just thinking English, Spanish, or any other written language; I am also thinking what shows up as an image in the mind. Also, a person's body language is very telling. The way a person carries themselves when they walk always reflects injuries or diseases they may suffer from. Since the physical eyes have so much to take in and figure out, the mind's eye is free to wander.

Without self-awareness or focus on what the mind's eye is looking at, any beauty the physical eyes see can get cancelled out by the mind's eye. The thing is, the mind's eye isn't bound to the truth that the physical eye sees. A person cannot always depend on what the physical eyes see either, due to the fact that the mind has the ability to fill in missing parts in order to create a whole picture. Not to mention some things are very good at creating illusion.

Seeing is believing most of the time. Just like night dreams seem so real, daydreams without attention become real. You see, since no one actually wants the negative, it can use trickery to exist. What I mean by this is, people who are down or depressed a lot may not even realize they dwell in a negative state of mind. When around these people, you may feel like they're sucking the life energy right out of you. It's because they are. I believe this could be because of the natural laws that govern power and energy in general.

People like myself who suffer from clinical depression are often given powerful drugs to increase dopamine and serotonin levels in the brain in order to elevate mood. These chemicals in the brain are what stimulate the connection or the pathways for the electrical pulses to activate the parts of the brain which affect our mood or makes us feel good or well. If a person quits doing the drugs, then, naturally, there will be a mood crash. I have found for me that thought of having to do a drug the rest of my life is depressing by itself. Not to mention all drugs have side effects.

I am no longer on medication; however, it is not a good idea to quit meds without a good medical person to help monitor you. If you have artificially been supplying the body with a needed chemical, the body will stop producing that chemical in order to self-monitor; or if you have lost an organ, which was responsible for producing a needed chemical, you can die. Though the medical field has come a long way, there is a reason why they call it medical practice.

Anyway, I have found what works for me is to be aware of the language I use when talking to myself and especially the language I use talking to others. I also have noticed when I am lacking the energy to carry on—no matter how good things are going in my life at the time—usually improves when I physically ground myself to the earth and literally let the sun shine on me. I mean, take your shoes and socks off and put your bare feet in the cool grass on the ground and allow the natural law which controls energy to seek the path of least resistance to ground.

Remember, the earth is the ultimate grounding source for all energy. The sun is nothing but energy which would fry us without the magnetic fields created by the positive and negative flow our beautiful spinning planet to protect us. This spinning allows the perfect balance of day and night so life can energize in the day and rest at night.

Depending on what you and your body desires or needs, the correct temperature and energy exposure can be achieved by where you live on the planet. We can jump on a plane and experience any climate we desire in a day. For those who like all the seasons, like myself, the tilt of the earth changes so we can experience all the seasons without having to move. To live in a place which experiences winter, spring, summer, and fall is how one comes to appreciate the beauty of life on this perfect situation our planet provides. If I need an energy boost in the winter, the best grounding point I have found is hugging a tree. Perhaps you are thinking, *Oh my god, a tree hugger.*

Perhaps you are a pro-lifer who supports the death penalty. Why do you call that conservative? How is it those claiming to be God-fearing Christians or part of any religion who believe it's okay to profit off the natural resources our planet contains—such as plant life, which, through photosynthesis, supplies us with our oxygen and scrubs the air of CO_2—call themselves conservatives? Then we have the liberal party who were the party that owned slaves back in the day.

It's kind of funny how extremism of any kind tends to cycle back on itself and somewhat loses the focus of an ideology that is rarely ideal for the survival yet supports the life for all the people we think it would. Maybe this is where the word *idiot* comes from. To me, if we choose to create the situation of "us and them," no matter the situation—whether it be politics, religion, race, sports, or any one of the many things—which cause a division of "us and them," we will naturally have conflict leading to extreme emotions.

Before any conflict, healthy or unhealthy, there is an exchange of language or words. Even conflicts we have within ourselves use the word of our native language. With the power and magic the word contains, a person can motivate people or themselves to create a world of heaven with all its glory to be or the deepest hell unimaginable. It is your choice whether you use the word as white or black magic.

A person also needs to be aware of the tone of their words or voice. With the correct tone, even bad news can be easier to give or take. If you can learn to communicate clearly and from a place of love and beauty, you can calm the negativity of most situations. The more you focus your physical eyes on the natural beauty in the world, the more beauty the mind's eye will focus on. Though the physical eyes have limitations to the physical dimension, the mind's eye has no limitations, which is cool. Through the mind is how we connect the spirit energy who some call God.

You can focus your mind's eye on everything or anything in the nonphysical dimension and/or this physical dimension. The only reason you can't find things that are right in front of you is because your mind's eye can think it is somewhere else. Just become aware of which focus you are using. Perhaps you don't see something that is right in front of you because you choose to see what the mind's eye can.

Have you ever been chopping vegetables thinking about something else—usually something you are agitated at—and watch yourself cut your finger? Then you think, *I can't believe I just did that!* Have you ever noticed how long the pain takes to set in? People sometimes will cut themselves on purpose in order to take the focus off mental pain. It is almost like physical pain trumps mental pain and the mind's eye can trump the physical eye.

Have you ever thought about this? If not, why not? Do you ever pay attention to the way you are constantly thinking or daydreaming? How often do you make mistakes at work because you are thinking about something—or, better yet, someone else—while you work?

Do you then tell your boss or blame the mistake on someone or something else? Then perhaps later you punish or scold yourself for doing so? Or perhaps you say to yourself, *Woohoo! I got away with that one!* This all happens while the person you blamed it on is plotting revenge against you. Then the war is on. Pretty soon, both of you are messing up the job.

Haven't you ever blamed someone else for your mistake? Little kids do it all the time, usually because they see adults do it or they fear the punishment. A person in prison who is labeled a snitch is usually killed for doing so. They can justify murder, however—heaven forbid—tell on someone.

It seems easier to me to just not do anything you don't want anyone to know about. Don't do the crime if you can't do the time. Perhaps you have heard this statement. This is why one needs to think things through. What I mean by "think things through" is, you have to look at all the ways an action can result in. Everything in life can go either direction. My favorite Native American saying is "Good judgment comes with experience—experience comes from bad judgment."

Words and symbols live in both the physical and the nonphysical dimensions. Words have the power to create worlds and they have the power to destroy worlds. All a word needs is your intention and attention. There are a lot of different languages and ways to use language—body language, signs, and gestures. How do you feel when you try to communicate with someone who doesn't know your language? Does it not depend on who is the minority? If you are the foreigner, then it is probably fear you experience. Therefore, people who don't understand your language will be fearful toward you.

The universal language is math. There is no doubt in my mind that binary code—zeros and ones like computers use for language—is how we will communicate with aliens. What? You don't believe in aliens? I heard they are already here. Why can't you believe other life is possible? We are constantly finding new life on this planet. Why not expand your mind? It is fun. Learning is fun.

Through the power of the word, we can learn anything we want, by reading books or nature. We have so much to learn from observing nature we can apply to our personal lives. Since our mind lives in the nonphysical dimension with memory, there is no limit to how many languages we can learn. The only thing limiting us is the time our body has on or in this world.

To me, when our brain gets older, it tends to misfire and loses the ability to connect with the nonphysical dimension. Why else call it *dementia?* Most answers to *why* are all in the words. Some of the happiest people in the world speak a language which have no words to describe certain feelings, and so they don't experience the feelings.

The power of the word needs to be realized. One only has to pay attention to Twitter or any of the media to see how fast things get blown way out of proportion. There are many trolls or people who take pleasure in creating chaos or putting people down. This is usually coming from those with their own insecurities or a self-righteousness who hide behind places where they get a sense of anonymity.

There is nothing more poisonous than gossip, so it is the worst "black magic" way of using language. Those who use it aren't even smart enough to realize it will always come back to haunt them.

Chapter 7

Why Can't I See the Truth?

It's like the Jack Nicholson line in the movie *A Few Good Men*. Tom Cruise is a young military attorney asking Jack for the truth. Jack, the five-star general, says with a firm and stern voice, "You can't handle the truth!"

I find it interesting and quite ironic a movie with actors and actresses playing pretend is searching for the truth. Even if this movie is supposed to be based on facts, it is only a rendition. I define *rendition* as a "remembrance with additions." The additions are to keep everyone's attention.

Do you ever wonder why we seem to want so much attention? Perhaps it is because we are always trying to justify something to ourselves. It has been said our wanting others to like us comes from primitive times when if one wasn't liked by others, they would be cast out. To be cast out in primitive times meant you would no longer have the safety, which is a product or result that comes from safety in numbers. It is safer to have more people to hunt and protect themselves from animals, other groups, or tribes.

Though that was important, then it doesn't apply to survival as much now. However, instinct is instinct. We still, to this day, wear many faces to try and get along with everyone where we really don't need to. A third of the people will like you anyway, a third will dislike you, and the other third could care less about you.

So, to not be anything but yourself all the time will confuse things. To pretend to be different will only attract people who are different than you truly are. To be true to yourself is to be yourself, which will attract those who are like you and, in turn, will be people you like. This also helps one to realize not everyone is being themselves, and you can see those through the feelings you feel when around them. To live your truth saves much energy you waste on pretending. To act in ways only to be accepted by others requires much more energy than to just be yourself.

How would you feel if I told you the truth is only true in the moment it happens? What if I told you that everyone's truths are different? What, are you calling me a liar? Do you ever get angry at someone who lies to you then turn around and tell a little white lie to someone else? I am glad a lie is a lie, no matter what color you bathe it in. However, if it is part of a fiction story, we call it okay.

Let's say, for instance, a friend asks you to pick them up in the morning because they need a ride for a job interview they have at 8:00 a.m. (We will call this friend Bill.) Due to the fact that Bill owes you money, you say, "Sure. I will pick you up at 7:20 a.m. so I can drop you off at 7:45, and since my job is only ten minutes from there, I will still be on time for my job that starts at 8:00 am."

"Perfect," Bill replies.

Then you ask, "Would you like me to call you earlier?" thinking to yourself Bill has not worked in a while so it might be hard for them to get out of bed.

"No thanks," Bill says, "I am pretty excited about this interview, so I will be up."

You say, "Okay, see you in the morning."

As you are driving home, you are thinking to yourself about the money Bill owes you so. This is why you agreed to give Bill a ride to the interview. Then *screech!* Another car pulls right in front of you, and *boom!* You run right into the back end of their car. You both stop and get out. Their car is fine; however, you have front-end damage.

This scared person starts apologizing. "I am so sorry! I was just in a hurry because of a sick family member who is dying at the hospital." They go on about the story of how they just want to get there in time to say sorry because the last time they spoke to the dying person, they told the person hateful things. We will name the speedster Boob. What's in a name? (Well, come to find out the name Boob is a nickname for a good friend of mine named Bob, so I apologized to Bob because he is anything but a careless boob.)

Your first thought might be that Boob here is probably making this whole story up. Not only that, but look at the front of your car! The lights are broken, and who knows what damage lies beneath the surface. Let us say you only have liability insurance, so it would have to be Boob's insurance to pay to fix your car. Hey, maybe it would even cover that piece that has been rattling since your run-in with a curb.

At this point, you confront Boob and ask, "Do you have insurance?"

Boob says, "It just expired, and I have not had the money to renew it."

Boob then states, "I will pay for the damage to your car. Please do not call the cops!"

Just then, an officer just passing by stops and turns on his lights. You think to yourself, *Poor Boob here is having a bad day.*

The officer, whom we will name Friend, gets out of his car and asks us for our license, registration, and proof of insurance. You go to your car to retrieve your license, registration, and insurance and stand by the damaged end of your car. As you watch Officer Friend and Boob talking, you can't help but assume that Boob is in trouble for no insurance.

Officer Friend comes to you, takes your documentation, and asks you what happened. You tell him, "I was cruising along at the speed limit when ol' Boob here ran a Stop sign and pulled right out in front of me."

Officer Friend asks, "Do you need a tow?"

You reply, "No thank you. It seems to be drivable."

Officer Friend states, "Pull your vehicle off the road," pointing to the side of the road. Then the officer returns to his car to fill out paperwork.

While waiting for Officer Friend, your mind wanders back to Bill, the person whom you promised to pick up in the morning. You might say to yourself, *Maybe Bill needs to find a new ride.*

As you are pulling your car to the spot Officer Friend directed you to, you find comfort in how your car seems to feel okay. Then you think to yourself, *I sure hope the broken lights are all that is wrong with my car.*

Then you get out to look a little closer at the damage. "Just a turn signal lens," you say to yourself. You reach in and turn the switch on and look with anticipation. Sure enough, the light flashes fine.

I wonder how much that lens will cost, you think to yourself. *I guess it doesn't really matter*, your thought continues. *It isn't my fault*, you think with confidence.

Officer Friend gets out of his patrol car and walks toward you. He asks, "Are you okay? Do you have any injuries?"

"No, I don't think so," you say.

Officer Friend hands you a form and says, "If your condition should change, you will need to document it in this accident report. Please fill this out and sign it here." He then walks over to Boob and hands him an accident report and a yellow copy of a citation. You feel sorry for Boob but realize at least his car seems okay.

Then you overhear Officer Friend say to Boob, "Tell your brother hello for me. Your brother is a good man, and he is in the right place." Boob gets in his vehicle and drives away.

A strange feeling of bewilderment begins building in your mind. Suddenly, all sorts of questions start to pop in your head.

Why did Boob get to leave?

You answer yourself, *Probably so he could get to the hospital. It must be Boob's brother in the hospital. I wonder if Boob's brother is a cop. That would explain why he didn't want to call the police.*

As you are pondering these things, Officer Friend walks to your car and hands you a red copy of a citation.

"Please read this and sign on the line at the bottom," Officer Friend states.

As you begin to read hoping that you have just been handed a warning, the words "Careless driving resulting in an accident" come into focus.

As a feeling of anger begins burning in your gut, you plead your case by stating something like, "But, Officer, Boob pulled out in front of me. He ran the Stop sign!"

Officer Friend states, "The way I see it, you were driving too fast or not paying attention. You ran into the back of his car, so you are at fault.

If you disagree with this decision or wish to challenge the citation, you have the right to do so in court on this day here."

As he points to the date on the ticket, he says, "Sign here and you may be on your way. Please drive safely." He then hands you the red copy of the ticket.

As you drive away, you feel anger racing through your body in the form of adrenaline. Your mind might start reeling through different angry thoughts like, *I am innocent! That cop was biased because Boob's brother is a cop!* Then all the couldas and wouldas turn into the fear of how much this ticket is going to cost and the realization he isn't going to pay for the damage.

Then again, perhaps you have come to completely different conclusions throughout the situation. Perhaps, if I change the name *you* in the story to *me*, it might make it more believable for you. The truth of the matter isn't important because it is a fictional story I just made up. However, the basis for the entire scenario is factual because I am sure this has happened in some way or other to somebody, somewhere, at some point in time. Just believing or not believing doesn't make it true or false.

Does the fact this could happen somewhere make it true? That depends on who you are and what you believe. The truth of any situation is in how you see it. If you are focusing with your mind's eye, you will miss the physical truth that lives outside the focus of your physical eyes. If you want to see the truth, you have to focus more with the physical eyes, along with the mind's eye.

Even though you can bounce back and forth between your mind's eye and your physical eyes, you can perceive many things at the same time. So why not enjoy the beauty of truth in this moment before the mind turns it into some fact for the judge to use either for or against you later? This little story I made up only contains one truth in my world. Boob is a nickname of a very good friend of mine named Bob.

Our species loves a good story because we are so good at making them up. If we believe the story to be nothing but the truth, we will protect it with our life. Do you ever wonder why this is? I have many theories on this; however, you will have to read another one of my *Why* books to learn those theories.

Have you ever been to a Bible study group? If not, you should experience at least one in your life. The comradery was rather nice and enjoyable. One of the studies I was part of was at 6:00 a.m. every Wednesday morning at a place of business where I subcontracted most of my business. It was all volunteer, so the ones who showed up regularly wanted to be there. It was ran by the boss when the chaplain from New Orleans wasn't available.

The retired chaplain was a very interesting man who also held a psychiatry practice along with his wife, and the boss kept him on retainer for his employees. The chaplain and I became very close and had a working relationship. I myself was baptized and raised Catholic.

I really found it interesting how different some people's interpretations were when studying and answering the worksheet questions. What was even more surprising to me was how much the wording was different from Bible to Bible, though the passages could be interpreted the same. I've come to find out changes happen all the time when different Bible companies make new editions. I learned this from another good friend who is an actual Bible salesman and says the King James is the one with the least edits.

The fact there is an Old Testament and a New Testament, to me, gives credence to contamination or changing of the word. The fact the Bible was put together by longtime enemy Constantine, who only allowed certain writings, should be scrutinized. Not only that, how do we know for sure the translation from Hebrew to English is correct? What happens when English doesn't have the correct word or way to explain a Hebrew word? This is why I have little faith in today's Bibles.

The connection I feel with spirit energy I term *god* has proven itself many times, if not daily. I have had and seen many things in life that are best described as divine intervention. Though I am sure there are many truths in the Bible, religion has gotten many things wrong.

The truth of the human species not knowing for sure who we are or why we are here is only proven by the horrible way we treat each other, not to mention by the way we treat Mother Earth. It seems to me we are the only species on this planet that doesn't know why it's here.

In time, as we learn through science and history, all the answers to why we are here will become evident. We only need to face the truth, which is alive and changing—the same as all life is evolving and changing. All we have to do is look at the beauty that is nature to know of something godlike being part of the missing piece science is always looking for. The knowing we are still learning and don't have the answers is how truth sets us free to learn the truth.

Chapter 8

The Need to Judge Our Judgment

Good judgment comes from experience. Experience comes from bad judgment. I don't know about you; however, most of my experience with judges has been full of guilt and fear. Most of the time, I was angry because I got caught. Usually it was for driving violations. It seems to me that the younger I had the more freedom I wanted from all law. I don't know about you, but my adolescence was filled with seeing what I could get away with. Let's just say I have a lot of experience with this.

In this day and age, one would consider me a troubled problem child. The quickest way to get me to do something was to tell me I couldn't. If I didn't like your reason why, then the quicker I would do it. Actually, the more convincing the reason to not doing something seemed to increase the challenge.

If not for self-inflicted wounds, we would have no problems. How do you feel about this statement? If you don't see the truth in this statement, you might want to question your belief system. Perhaps the judge in you says some things we can't control. Though this is true, it has nothing to do with self-control. If you are lacking in self-control, then more often than not, you might struggle with addictive tendencies. Addiction causes many personal problems which create fear in all the people involved.

The definition of a *judge* has three different parts that are confusing.

The first definition is, "A public officer who decides cases in law." Remember, this only has to do with man's law. It has nothing to do with nature's law or God's law, which is unquestionably absolute. You cannot change the law of gravity, so it is justice.

The second definition goes, "A person who decides the results of a competition." I am afraid there is little room for conflict here. People think it is better to make rules so that the competition is fair. Yeah right! All is fair in love and war.

The third definition, we read, "A person with the necessary knowledge or skill to give an opinion." This definition I like the best for the fact the word *opinion* is all that a person has in comparing one person to another.

I like the saying "Opinions are like assholes—everybody has one!" Perhaps this statement brings out the judge in you. How have you been about judging yourself? I am not so sure since I struggle with my own self-judgment, which means I can truly rely on someone else's judgment of me.

How often is your opinion of yourself truly correct? How can I judge someone I don't even know? How often do we pass judgment on someone we don't know because of someone else's opinion? Have you ever said something bad about one person to another person out of anger for the first person? How many times have you been absolutely, positively sure of something because it came from a reliable source? Do you consider yourself a reliable source? If not, why not? If so, why?

Be honest with yourself. An important key to life is learning to be honest with yourself. A person who isn't honest with themselves won't be honest with other people.

How can anyone else have more knowledge about you than you do? How can you know what is best for someone else when you are not even sure what is best for yourself? How often do you punish yourself for your own self-judgment? How often do you do things just for the fun of it? Do you ever feel you are selfish? Perhaps you look at me as being selfish. Is being selfish a bad thing to you? If so, why?

What I am getting at here is, if one is giving things away to gain attention or to become accepted by a certain group or ideology, in my eyes, is still an act of selfishness. Any action requires a motive and or intent, which can be either positive or negative.

If the consequences of an action can take your freedom, why do it? If something is only fun if you get away with it, you don't understand what fun is. If something is only fun because it scares you, then you probably can relate to the statement "It is better to be lucky than good."

You probably use the statement "I am not afraid of anything." You probably even believe rules are made to be broken. You may believe good guys finish last, eye for an eye, and there is no justice in this world. You might even go so far as to say, "The only good politician is a dead politician." You would maybe even say the same thing about lawyers until you need one to fight for your freedom. Does the statement "I enjoy my freedom from behind my locked doors" make you laugh or make you angry? How would you define *freedom*? Do you believe you live in a free country?

If you agree with any of the last statements, your life may be based on fear. Is not the only place that we are free in the mind where thought occurs? If you are a good, God-fearing Christian, then perhaps you either look forward to Judgment Day, or you think you are most likely bound for hell so why not have fun until then. This all sounds justifiable to me.

Not only that, as long as one accepts Jesus Christ as Lord and savior on their deathbed, all sins are forgiven. If this is true, where is the justice in that? Perhaps this is the very reason we feel the need to punish each other while we are here. Perhaps you are thinking I have something against religion, so you feel the presence of your "inner judge." Aren't Muslims, Jews, and Christians worshipping the same god?

Though there are many positive things that come out of religion, there are also many negative things religions create. There is much war in the world based on different religious beliefs. It seems to me we are all knocking on the same door.

Man has been making up rules and laws to control or govern each other for thousands of years. The Ten Commandments were pretty much to the point and simple to follow; however, it wouldn't matter if there were only one rule. Not everyone cares to follow the rules, no matter how much sense they make. There is no way to change anyone's mind but your own. Why try to force beliefs or ideas on people who don't want to believe them? It seems to me that human nature is to push back when pushed on. If you live by example and your example leads to a life of serenity and joy, other people will naturally want to know why and how you have achieved this life of satisfaction.

Have you ever defined what a sin is? I like the definition of *sin* as being anything one does or says that goes against oneself. Any action or verbalization you do to someone else that makes them dislike or seek revenge against you is a sin.

This also includes you talking bad about yourself to yourself or anyone else. This includes doing anything that hurts you, like abusing drugs, oversmoking, overeating, over-anything. This helps me understand the sin thing in a common-sense sort of way. This also creates room for the punishment from sinning to happen in the now instead of something that comes on a judgment day.

Is not every day a judgment day for oneself? Do we not punish ourselves on a daily basis? What if Jesus died because of our sins, not to forgive our sins? There is a lot of room for misunderstanding in the Christian Bible. Humans are so easily confused and controlled by emotion.

Please do not misunderstand me here. I am not against or for religion or politics. I am more for not putting all my faith in any one thing for the simple reason it was said to be truth. I have found that putting too much effort in seeking something always leads me to finding something. However, rarely does that something turn out to be true.

As soon as I put my faith in something, then I become judgmental about it. As soon as I become judgmental about it, I think I am an authority on it. As soon as you are sure you know all about something, you stop learning about it to some extent.

I have found, when I attempt to teach from an authoritative angle, things happen to let me know how much I still need to learn. When I teach from the angle of helping another person figure it out, we both end up learning from each other. Since the truth is alive and always changing, the only way to know the truth is to live in the moment truth lives in, which is right now. That might not even be true. Why we are always searching for the truth is because it makes us feel safe. The only truth we need is our own truth.

To me, judgment is best used as a way to gauge whether or not an action was truly joyful. Judgment should only be used to help oneself learn about the importance of life. There is no doubt in my mind a life energy of God exists—which creates all that is and all that is born—

in the form of ideas or critters, human and nonhuman. Though this is a belief that works for me, what works for you may be a completely different set of principles.

If I judge you for your set of principles, you will judge me for mine. This then slows us both from learning the truth, which is bad judgment. Since the truth almost always comes out, why not observe where it comes from instead of where it might be hiding?

More often than not, the truth is right in front of us; however, we choose not to see it for one reason or another. Perhaps we don't want to be the bearer of bad news. Why do we feel we can protect anyone from bad news? Why do we feel the need to judge everything in life, from the way our food tastes to the clothes other people wear?

Let us all experience the learning process without judgment, and the truth will absolutely set us free. We will be free to learn all the truth that life is, with help from each other and without judgment. To me, God—being what all energy consists of—gives me a presence of God I can see and feel. So many people rely on religious beliefs to guide them through life and live with the fear that God will punish them now and in the end. God doesn't have to punish man because man punishes himself in the name of God.

Perhaps God doesn't judge at all, due to the fact that for life to continue along with creation, God only needs to be the energy which makes it all possible. After all, is it not oneself who is the hardest judge to appease? As long as we allow other people to call the shots and make rules to live by, there will be conflict and confusion with others as well as within ourselves. Perhaps fear is the only thing that makes us judge, so fear is where I am going next.

Chapter 9

Why Fear Is so Important

Please understand, though some of this is repetitive, we often will gain more perspective through repetition. "We have nothing to fear but fear itself"—have you ever thought about the truth of this statement? Do you ever contemplate or anticipate an action that may cause fear? How often does the action turn out to not warrant the feeling of fear you experienced?

To me, *fear* is the most powerful four-letter word in the English language. I could go on and list many labels of things we fear. However, isn't fear best described as an emotion? Do you label fear as good or bad or perhaps both? How can something be good and bad at the same time? Fear is a reaction that is supposed to lead to self-preservation, is it not?

What do you think about fear? Is it something to avoid or overcome? Do you ever question why you might be afraid of something? Anytime you feel jealousy, anger, sadness, or depression—it is usually due to fear. Though fear is very important in the preservation of one's life, it is also a most powerful thing that keeps one from getting all one wants out of life.

How much faith do you put in superstitions? Did you know we create most everything bad or good that happens to us through the law of attraction? Therefore, most things one fears will come to happen. The stronger you believe, the more energy you give it. The more energy you give it, the more life energy it attracts. The universe doesn't look at positive or negative energy as bad or good. There is just a law that keeps life energy flowing and cycling. Without it, life would just stop. It is all about the energy.

Did you know that if someone were to tell you that you have a patch of brown skin that looks like cancer, if you believe this person and fear it enough, chances are, you will have cancer within one year? Have you ever been handling something fragile and someone warns you to be careful? With this statement, the fear of breaking the object enters your mind, and *poof*, you drop it or break it. It is like some strange force comes out of nowhere and causes you to lose control.

Perhaps you know someone who is always sick. Even receiving a vaccination makes them sick. Sometimes, though vaccines shouldn't make you sick, the psychological power of fear creates a feeling of being ill. If you fear getting sick, which is a type of faith in the sickness, you will get sick. Just like if you are sure you will get well, you have faith in healing, so you will get well.

If you are sure you will get scared of something, you get scared. Have you noticed when someone is deathly afraid of something like dogs or spiders, maybe even due to an allergic reaction they want to avoid, the dog or spider makes a beeline straight for that person? It is the law of attraction. It is like what we fear the most is continually presented to us until we learn how to deal with it.

Once we understand we can deal with something we are afraid of, then it becomes fun to deal with, like swimming or riding a horse or driving a vehicle. Once we understand the law of attraction, the more we practice it, the better we become at it; and then the more fun we have with it. When we face our fears and it doesn't bring harm, it feels good.

The same holds true with the thoughts in the mind. We have so many things we fear that are nothing but nonphysical thought energy. We often try to avoid these fearful thoughts with drugs or other actions, but the harder we try to avoid it, the more power we give it to continue. A fine quote from the animated movie *Kung Fu Panda* is, "One often meets his destiny on the road he takes to avoid it!"

How often have you thought about a time when you were sick so you think about how to avoid getting sick again when, at the moment, you are not sick at all? Why waste your thought energy on that? It is much better to focus your thought energy on feeling good right now.

A big reason we turn to drugs or other addictive behaviors is to avoid certain thoughts or the fear of feeling something. Focusing on doing what makes you happy and healthy will bring you the positive energy necessary to create a life of joy and bliss. This way of thinking takes practice, the same as everything else we do in life.

Perhaps it appears I have been focusing on the negativity in life more than the positive. This is only because so many times, the things we fear or don't like stand out in our thoughts. What I would like you to do is become aware of what you are thinking about first and then think why you are thinking what you're thinking about. Where does this thought come from? A place of fear or a place of want and desire?

We fear what we know. We fear what we don't know. We fear losing things we have. We fear not having enough. We waste a whole lot of energy on worrying about this or that when we have all the power of the universe at our disposal to create a completely bountiful and joyous life. Without a little positive action to create a positive life, the natural default has to be negative. No one intentionally lives a negative life, unless negative actions feel good to them. There always has to be some who are wired differently. Right or wrong is only relative to one's beliefs.

Perhaps you fear death. Dying seems to me to be the easiest part. It is living that is the hard part! The reason we fear death perhaps is because we are not sure what to believe about it.

There are many people who have died and come back, and most of them say the same thing. They usually talk about floating above their bodies and experiencing total peace without pain or worry, and most of the time they would prefer not to come back. They usually experience floating toward a bright light where they meet someone who was very close to them who died earlier. This person tells them it is not their time and they need to go back for some reason. The reason, most often, has to do with another person still living, like a child in need of their guidance. There are also those who experience a hellish and tormenting-type presence who often come back to be a better and more considerate person.

Do you ever question yourself as to why you fear dying? Is it because you fear the fire of hell? Perhaps you fear the pain you will feel before death sets in. Maybe you fear what will happen to others who are depending on you.

Personally, I have died a couple of times due to drug overdose. I did not have an out-of-body experience. However, there was no pain. Even though I required CPR to bring me back, perhaps I was not dead long enough to see the things others report. Maybe it was because the drugs affected my memory. I most likely experienced many things but do not remember in my conscious mind. I must have experienced something.

Though it took some time, I have changed. It affected me. My subconscious seems to remember. It really doesn't matter what you believe because what is really important is the here and now. There is no way to change the past, and the future may not even get here, so why not enjoy and nurture the fact that you probably have many years ahead so make the best of them?

If you were told you only have one week to live, what would you do? Would you lie around and say, "Poor me," or would you try to make the best of it? I am pretty sure you wouldn't care what anyone else thought. If you are a drug addict and you knew you were dying anyway, you would be happy for a change. Since you are just slowly killing yourself anyway, this would give you an understandable excuse.

I find that most people don't do or try new things because they may be afraid of doing it incorrectly or because they fear the embarrassment of not understanding or knowing the rules. Even people who find it fun to steal or rob enjoy the part fear plays in the action. Though it takes practice to be a successful thief, a thief is just a thief, and they always get caught sooner or later.

I have lived at or below the poverty level most all my life. I usually say I am very rich, just not very wealthy. I am rich in knowledge, love, and have been blessed in the way of finding my God-given talent, which is welding.

The poor steal because they believe it is the only way they can get their needs met. The poor usually stay poor because they fear not having what it takes to be anything else. So, they fall victim to accepting their life as what it is. Is it not a lack of knowledge or the knowing there is another way? Or is it the beliefs one thinks to be true? I can only have what I know how to get.

The only reason we have what we have is because we believe this is all we can have or achieve. You cannot do anything you say you can't. We absolutely attract what we say and think. It is the law of attraction. We get what we believe, good or bad. The ability to read and write is huge in escaping poverty; it is the lack of education or knowledge which creates most of the economic divide.

The fear a mother has of losing a child can stimulate great amounts of physical power and strength, like lifting a car off a crushed child. Even a small animal will exhibit great power when protecting their young from a predator. Even though we say the reaction the mother had come from fear when a boost of adrenaline gave her the power to lift the car, I am not so sure this is the case. It seems to me that the action happened so fast, the thought process doesn't have time to inter*fear*. We are very close to having the same makeup of chimpanzees. However, they are two times stronger than humans.

Is not the fact that the small animal shows no fear when protecting its young from a predator the reason that the predator backs down? Therefore, isn't the thought of—or the fear of—getting hurt shifted to the predator? It seems to me that the predator then becomes the one who is fearful or afraid. So perhaps fear is just a type of controlling thought that is part of instinct for self-preservation.

Though one can't stop fearful thoughts, they can become aware of these thoughts which stimulate a sense of fear. If you know why, then you can move to the action of how or what to do. If you know what to do, the fear pretty much goes away.

When I went through my EMT training, I was amazed on how a few of the most squeamish people became completely opposite after learning the procedure to administering medical attention in an emergency medical situation. I have a friend who was deathly afraid of needles when we started our EMT training and is now an anesthesiologist who does things like spinal taps in order to do nerve blocks for surgeries. We are talking big needles directly into the spine where one little mistake can permanently paralyze.

To become educated about things we fear most always changes the action we fear, doing into an action we enjoy doing. There is nothing like a little fear to make one focus with both your mind's eye and your physical eyes, not to mention all your senses. Total concentration with your whole being usually always leads to a successful action, which in turn will restore the energy you normally lose to being afraid. You will find when you are completely focused on an action the fear goes away.

Most of the fear we have about death comes from making assumptions. Do we not just fear the pain that we believe must precede death? The thing I have learned about pain is that usually when it is severe enough, one goes into shock or passes out.

I have experienced a crushed foot, broken bones, burnt eyes, and quite a few other physical traumas. The fear doesn't usually arise until after the action is done. Then both the pain and the fear of how much damage is done comes to mind.

It is like I wonder if it is damaged for life or will it heal. Medical professionals get better at fixing the human body all the time. They use 3D printers to make new body parts now. It is mostly patches of skin for skin grafts now. However, one can only believe it will be all organs in time with the development of stem cell.

Mostly the printers are used on prosthetics. Working prosthetic arms and legs are all the rage with the injured soldiers we have from another decade of war. There are a multitude of medical breakthroughs due to the practice and research resulting from the injuries war produces. One can look at war as being very profitable, not to mention it does help the overpopulation. Some people of power justify war in this way. How and why do you personally justify war? Perhaps it is to allow us our freedom. During the draft, those called don't have the freedom to opt out.

We are so hypocritical and easily manipulated by fear. I often wonder why we think it's a bad thing to show fear. Is it not because of vulnerability we connect with being afraid? Does not all war start because of fear? To have the biggest, most powerful army and bombs in the world hasn't saved us from war. Throughout history, to be the most powerful is the very thing that creates a target for war. Or is it the fear the biggest and baddest have of being overcome so they start picking on others to confirm their power?

No one likes a bully, and the underdog wins because of fight or flight, a reaction that gains more power when backed into a corner. Does not the underdog team win because (1) they believe they can win do to realizing a weakness in the big dog and (2) they have all the nonphysical energy coming from those praying and cheering them on?

To protect one's own shores is one thing; to meddle on others is only asking for trouble, even when it seems morally justified. It doesn't matter who's right or wrong when both sides views themselves as heroes and the other side as the enemy. We are all just humans, so the emotional scars always last long after the soldiers are gone.

It is too bad they have not figured out how to deal with the emotional trauma. We lose more soldiers to suicide than we do in the actual battles. Mental pain brings on a fear that is much trickier to deal with. The military brainwashes a soldier into believing that is it more honorable to die in battle for a cause or your fellow man than it is to survive. So, if they are lucky enough to live through it, they come back with this feeling of guilt or shame because they didn't die.

If one believes that the only hero is the one who dies on the battlefield, then how can one help but feel dishonorable for living? I personally will never ask or expect anyone to die for me. I would much rather die to save others than the other way around, especially since I view death as a natural part of the life cycle. To me, death is just a transfer of energy from the physical form to the nonphysical form. From what I have learned, I tend to believe in reincarnation and the physical body our spirit lives in was by choice. I think we just forgot why we chose this life.

All the people I know who have taken someone's life do not go through even one day that they don't think about the person they killed. Most of them seem to fear any enjoyment of life because they believe they do not deserve it. I have a friend who was in Vietnam and really liked what he did over there. He did not want to come back. After he did come back, the only way he could seem to enjoy life was to put himself into life-or-death situations. He went to hauling drugs in hopes of finding the ones who wanted to keep both the drugs and the money. It took that kind of fear to make him feel alive.

This man happens to be the person who saved me by performing CPR on me when I overdosed on drugs. I was so grateful that I wanted to return the favor. So, what did I do? I tried to overdose him so I could save him. After I got to the point of giving him twice the dose it took to kill me and couldn't kill him, I gave up. How is that for messed-up thinking?

Perhaps the more one fears death, the easier death comes. It's not like he was that much bigger than I was. I should have had a higher tolerance due to the fact that I used more drugs than he did. I know this to be true because we lived and worked together at the time.

The only thing which makes sense to me is, he was better at dealing with fear. I believe perhaps the adrenaline that rushes through the body when one fears death so much possibly stops the heart. Maybe that is what scared to death means! It is like the guy who dies of a heart attack when he falls from a great height. He was probably dead before he hit the ground.

The truth of the saying "What doesn't kill you makes you stronger" is very logical in many ways. To fear death is healthy. To be afraid of something you think is scary but won't necessarily kill you isn't healthy. To let your fear of fear stop you from living life will most likely shorten your life.

Perhaps you are a God-fearing Christian who believes in heaven and hell when we die. Why worry when all you have to do is accept Jesus Christ as your lord and savior? Then all the evil and bad things you've done in life are magically pardoned. How convenient is that, especially when you can do it on your deathbed? I am sorry if I am picking on Christians, but it is only because I was raised in the Catholic Church. Though the Bible study included people from other churches, it is still considered Christian.

From my life experience, I have seen more things to fear about religion and the churches. I have seen too many bad things happen to good people and good things happen to bad people. All the religions preach how good God is and at the same time doing horrible things to his fellow man. Does this not allow room for God to be both good and evil? This is why the whole "God is just the life energy which makes all of life possible" hypothesis works for me.

This still allows room for good and bad angels lurking in the nonphysical dimension where spirit energy (God) can influence the physical dimension through the minds of all the living things throughout the entire universe that requires the electron (God) to create the physical universe. This is because the protons and neutrons powered by the electron or power of God make up the physical universe as we know it. God is the radio wave, and our brain is the antenna and physical part of our body that houses the soul and mind where nonphysical and physical energy (God) meet. The angels of life and death continually try to maintain the balance that is life, through positive and negative.

I have learned to embrace the angel of death. Since the angel of death takes away the old so the new can live, then why not give the angel of death all those old thoughts which create fear so that you can nurture new thoughts of life? When I look at the fear soldiers endure, it makes my fear of not being good enough or my fear of failed relationships rather petty in comparison. If fear comes from thinking, then it is based on the assumption that something might happen. Really then, fear only has power if you give it power. With this said, why not focus your power on the good you can create in the now and let the angel of death take and free you from the past?

The best thing about the past is that is it done and over with, so let it go and focus on your life in the now. It just takes a little practice. You will enjoy solving new problems in life when you refocus the energy you have been wasting on the old problems you cannot change. Make use of the Serenity Prayer: "God grant me the serenity to accept the things I cannot change, the courage to change the things I can, and the wisdom to know the difference."

If what I fear can't kill me, why fear it at all?

Chapter 10

Why We Are All Addicted

The word *addict*, according to *Merriam-Webster*, is defined as "to devote or surrender [oneself] to something habitually or obsessively." Why does one become addicted? I believe addictions come from doing something that brings comfort. If just being devoted to an action, like saving the world or something like that, is an addiction, then we are all addicted to something.

It is human nature to find comforting things, especially during uncomfortable times. It starts when we are very young. A baby cries and the mother feels uncomfortable, so she plugs a pacifier or a bottle into the baby's mouth or gives the baby its favorite blanket. Most of the time, this calms the baby and then it's off to the next chore.

Usually, the little person gets older and grows out of the need to drag around its blanket or suck on something. All babies of the warm-blooded variety are born with the instinct to suck. This is another law of nature that is just built in for the survival of the species. Could you imagine if the adults had to teach their babies how to suck? That would suck!

I heard a story of a lady who adopted a small blind baby who was born severely challenged. Even though this baby was born without vision and the natural reflex of sucking, this wonderfully determined woman took to helping this little baby. She taught it how to suck by caressing its little cheeks and making sucking noises. This poor little blob couldn't even walk. It had to drag itself around with its arms. Turns out, this little person is a piano savant with perfect pitch.

One late night, the woman woke up to piano music, thinking the TV or radio was left on, only to find the little one playing songs it had heard earlier on the radio. She wasn't sure how this little person even dragged itself to the piano, even up on the bench to play it. Things like this tend to make me think we are all born with a God-given talent or purpose for life.

What this says to me is we all have a purpose or something we like to do. When we have interest or enjoy an action, we do it over and over again. If it makes us feel good or takes our mind off the things in life we fear, it is very likely to become a habit or an addiction.

Everything else we learn in life comes from the practice of repeating an action over and over. It then becomes a habit. The way we teach any animal or baby is through repetition. When the person or animal does what we want, we reward them with an "attaboy" or a treat. If they don't want to do what we want, we punish them with a "bad boy" or a "bad girl" statement. This is the process of domestication.

Once domesticated, we take it upon ourselves to reward ourselves for being good or we judge and punish ourselves for bad behavior. When we get older, sometimes the things we reward ourselves with makes the nonphysical mind feel good but is not necessarily good for the physical body. Sometimes, food for the soul conflicts with food for the body. If one can get addicted to things that are feeling good to both the mind and body, then a life of happiness is the result. Though drugs can make both the mind and body feel good and happy, the reality of something which damages the physical body can never end in happiness.

The nonphysical thought energy in the mind is eternal, and it carries the power that controls the physical body. Once a thought controls the mind, the body has to follow. Once you become aware, you can choose what to think about, and then you regain control of your mind and the body follows. The problem with the power of nonphysical thought energy is the act of trying not to think about something and only adding to its power—"I think, therefore I am."

The only way to change what you are thinking about is to change or replace the thought. This takes practice. However, it gets easier with repetition.

Let's say you are a smoker. Do you ever not think of quitting these days? Perhaps not, so why not? They are pretty pricey. You could reward yourself well with something that satisfies both the mind and body with all the money you would save not buying cigarettes.

Let's say you are dying for a smoke, which is kind of an oxymoron. If you can take the focus off the cigarette and place it on another action or task at hand, then the urge will subside. This will only happen if you make it a point to enjoy the action or task at hand. The problem here is, you need to come up with a new reward other than a cigarette. I found that regular gum helped me substantially. I believe anything with nicotine in it prolongs the agony since it's the chemical the body craves.

It is funny how the mind usually rewards itself with something harmful to the physical body. Maybe it is because the mind knows the freedom it has to roam the universe if it wasn't restricted or trapped in the physical dimension of this life, which this body holds it to. Perhaps, this is why the mind is constantly trying to escape in daydreams.

I must be losing my mind! Okay, let's smoke and feel better. Maybe I will poison myself with sweets before I smoke. Oh god! My mind is trying to kill me! How is that for conspiracy? The mind wants to kill the physical body so it can be free to wander the universe.

Okay, let's come back to earth or, at least, to the world in which we have to live—mind, body, and spirit. It seems to me the root of our addictions is in the mind wanting comfort, so why not look at what makes the mind uncomfortable? Perhaps it has something to do with the confusion the whole world seems to be in the state of. Maybe you have mental pain or guilt from self-judgment. It probably has to do with all the above. It takes thirty days to create a habit, so it will take thirty days to break one.

I know a lot about drug addiction from personal experience. I have seen and lost many things because of my drug addictions. Though drugs were my biggest downfall, many people struggle with sex, gambling, alcohol, prescription drugs, video games, horse and dog racing—pretty much anything that creates problems in your life you can't stop doing or don't want to stop, though you know you should.

Humans are creatures of habit, whether the habits are good or bad. If the habits or addictions are healthy, we tend to praise the people who have them or even envy their devotion. Those who are workaholics, whether bodybuilders or businesspersons, are just as addicted as the person on the street we call a junkie.

The truth of the matter is, too much of any one thing is not good. A person who can find the balance in life, which includes a variety of habits—some of exercise, work, and play, along with the rest or sleep their body requires—will live a long, mostly joyous life. The eating habits and environment are also very important.

Though everyone knows this, it's not as easy as it sounds. The reason why we don't follow a regimen of healthy habits, I believe, can be attributed to boredom or a lack of excitement. We do better or enjoy things that stimulate us. Fear can be very stimulating and causes the body to release adrenaline, which gives us the power for fight or flight.

People who run a lot for long distances experience what is termed "a runners high," due to the release of endorphins. Chemicals in the form of pills, powder, or liquids we call drugs cause the brain to release serotonin, dopamine, and other chemicals, which makes us feel euphoric or happy, maybe even aroused. Some drugs like opioids, morphine, and heroin work because they block pain receptors in the brain and also have a calming effect.

These days, we have a pill for whatever ails you. They appear magical in the way your body feels. The problem with this is that what goes up, must come down, as the saying goes. When you introduce a chemical into the body—which, in turn, triggers the release of chemicals in the brain making you feel better or high, if you will—the brain and body will self-regulate the production of the chemical the drug triggers the release of. Hence the need to take more of the drug in volume to achieve the same feeling or high.

Just a little of the drug taken in the beginning turns into needing more. We call this the process of building immunity to the drug. We become immune to the drug, which is only half the problem. You see, the drug was causing the brain to release a chemical our body makes on its own naturally. So, the body becomes chemically dependent on the drug in order to make the natural chemical which, when released, makes the body feel normal or good.

Okay, now you take the drug out of the picture. The brain was relying on the drug to tell it when to make and release the feel-good chemical. The brain then doesn't produce or release the natural chemical, and the body goes into what we call *withdrawal*. This makes you one sick individual, depending on the drug you stop taking.

Different drugs have different withdrawal symptoms. Drugs tend to have either an upper or downer affect. Some people will do uppers in the morning to wake up and downers at night to sleep. These people really get sick if they stop, some actually die. Though alcohol is the one drug that can kill you the easiest in withdrawal, it's the only one that is legal. Heroin withdrawals make you very sick, with lots of muscle pain and cramps, but it usually won't kill you.

Depending on the drug you have been using and for how long determines how long your body feels sick, and even more significant is how long it takes the brain to return to the natural production of the chemical the drug was simulating. I know, for me, I was very dependent on speed or methamphetamine, which I used to get off cocaine dependency. Addicts will often substitute one drug for another to keep from getting sick.

We usually have a drug of choice; however, I wanted anything that pepped me up. When you become chemically dependent, the cost of drugs keep you broke, so you don't have time to stop and be sick, if you still have a job. So, you are "living to use and using to live," which is one of many clever sayings found in the Narcotics Anonymous book.

This program saves lives every day and taught me more than any of the many state programs I was forced to pay for. Let me put it to you this way: I started huffing gas at six years old and overdosed on alcohol at ten. I started on the needle at twelve and thirteen and didn't have more than a few days straight until I was in my midforties. So, when it comes to drug addiction, I have a little bit of experience.

After I finally got clean, it took me a good year to have any sense of what normal feels like. I ended up with hepatitis C, which I still have and have had it for many years now. Though there is a new drug that cures 95 percent of the people with this disease, it costs a thousand dollars a pill and requires a pill a day for twelve weeks. The way I feel about the pharmaceutical companies is lower on the pole than most of the drug dealers on the street. Some are still my friends, even if they are still struggling with their addictions.

The ones on the street don't have to push because most of them can't keep up with demand and only sell to supply their own habit. The pharmaceutical companies advertise on TV and mark up their drugs, sometimes as much as 15,000 percent. The large drug cartels don't have to push the drugs because they can't keep up with the demand. Doctors prescribe addictive drugs, and people get addicted and find that street drugs are cheaper and easier to get and overdose because of not knowing the potency, which varies substantially.

Anyway, there is life after addiction; and if you put in the time to allow your body to heal and balance its chemicals in the brain, the good feeling I experience now naturally is higher and better than any high I ever got from drugs. I overdosed and died twice in one week. So, I know what *high* feels like.

To beat an addiction happens one day at a time, and the ones who die usually have beat it for a while. Then they start feeling good when something mentally stressful happens, or they just miss the routine and they do too much and overdose because their body doesn't have the immunity it once had. You see, the routine and the act of doing the drugs become an addiction in and of itself. Many times, one experiences a high just from the anticipation of getting and doing the drug. If you are struggling with an addiction or trying to help a loved one with an addiction, there are many NA, AA, or Al-Anon meeting rooms internationally that will be happy to see you, take you in, and help you find the tools needed to recover from any addiction.

The biggest problem with addiction is, if the addict doesn't want to stop. He or she won't stop until the body forces the mind to stop. You can do an intervention and force the person into treatment, but they usually go right back after they get out. More often than not, an addict is trying to numb or not feel some type of pain, whether mental or chronic physical pain.

If a person doesn't know or understand why and where the pain comes from, drugs or anything that numbs or distracts from the pain can become a habit or an addiction. Sometimes the true source of the pain can be very illusive. This can be because the body can develop "pain memory" where it still hurts long after the physical injury has healed and should no longer hurt. People who have lost limbs often experience ghost pain in parts of the limb no longer there. Can you imagine the frustration of feeling your hand cramp to the point it feels like your fingernails are tearing holes in your palms on an arm that is no longer even there?

There is a doctor who got an idea to use a mirror to help this individual. He would use the reflection of his right arm to appear as the left arm in the reflection and would imagine the left-hand opening, while he was looking at his right hand opening in the mirror, and the pain completely went away. After repeating this several times at home, the pain didn't come back. However, he now has the sensation of fingers hanging from his shoulder where the arm was attached. It doesn't hurt, so it's not a bother. Normally, a doctor would prescribe powerful opioids with all the side effects and depression which goes along with them, to no avail.

This bears credence to my getting to the root of the pain by going into the "mind which controls the brain which controls the body" theory of mine. We have continuous beliefs and unconscious beliefs. Root out the mental part in pain, and there is no need to self-medicate or do drugs for the pain. It is truly amazing what power thought has.

The mind is where the power of thought energy can heal pretty much anything you put your mind to. Once you understand the physical *why* we are addicted, it makes it much easier to control any addiction. Sometimes, the meetings themselves turns into the healthy habit, and to see new people coming into the rooms are a needed, constant reminder of the suffering addictions cause.

To go back to an addiction after one learns the tools to recover is termed *relapse* and often leads to overdose or death. This happens because the self-judgment and guilt one feels is magnified because of the understanding of knowing *how* and *why* we become addicted in the first place. To be complacent often leads to tough times, whether an addiction or just not taking care of your own life.

Chapter 11

Practice Makes the Master

Practice makes perfect, they say. As soon as one learns the practice of playing the life game is only as fun as we make it, then one learns how to enjoy all one practices. It is all in how you choose to look at it.

When I find myself in a practice I don't care to do, the first thing I do is ask myself *why* I am in this predicament. That question is always answered with, "If it weren't for self-inflicted wounds, we would have no problems." Then I can focus on the task at hand and plan the work. Work is only unpleasant if you don't particularly care or enjoy doing it. So, plan the work and work the plan. I always love it when a plan comes together. As long as you do the best you can, your inner judge will not bother you.

It is always better to practice playing something you enjoy to the point you get paid for it. You will find most of the high-paid athletes knew at a very young age what they wanted to play. However, the physical body usually gets pretty worn out at earlier ages as well. Everything is best with a little moderation.

Another saying I find truth in is "A person can't have too many skills." This is not to be mistaken for the "jack of all, master of none" person. I find until you learn what it takes to master a skill, you struggle with all practices of life. The saying that states "It is better to have loved and lost than not to have loved at all" is what the jack-of-all-trades says—for the simple fact, if you can't master something, then you might not know love. It is said that it takes ten thousand hours to master something.

In order to master any sort of play, one has to learn how to convert the nonphysical mind energy into physical energy, which moves all the muscles of the body. This takes, sometimes, a lot of repetition to make the flow of energy smooth. Once a skill is mastered, you no longer have to waste any energy on the thought process because it becomes reflex. Once it becomes reflex, then the mind is free to focus on any one or all the steps of the action.

To master something, it takes seeing an action in your mind's eye and turning that into the exact action you see your body do through your physical eyes. You can pretty much conquer anything you put your mind to. However, you can't do anything you say you can't.

Let's use throwing something for an example. If you practice throwing a ball or a dart, you first must pay attention to pretty much every step as you go through all the motions. First, you might think about the grip. Then you decide overhand or underhand. Then you work on how to swing the forearm. Then you work on the release from your hands. Then you might start to focus on swinging your upper body and try to time the swing of your upper body, which leads to the shoulder, which leads to the upper arm to the forearm to the release with the hand.

Each of these steps are practiced over and over until it turns into pretty much one fluid motion. After enough practice, you find that in order to hit a target, most of your focus is on the wrist and the release. Pretty soon, you just look at what you want to hit, and, *boom*, you make the connection. With continued practice, soon, you are on target more and more.

This is because through muscle memory, you get to where you can look at a target and hit it without having to focus on the actual throwing action. The master comes to a point where they know why an action will happen and how it will happen. This is also a good example of nonphysical thought energy being converted to physical or kinetic energy.

After you become well practiced at an action, it becomes easier and more fun. It doesn't matter what the action is. Once you start enjoying it, it becomes fun. The more fun it is, the better you get at it, and so the more you want to practice it.

After about thirty days, it becomes habit. Once something becomes habit, the action doesn't require much focus, so the mind is free to wander and think about other things. However, if there are other thoughts going on which strike the fear emotion, like something in your life that is bothering you, your game will suffer.

This fear will often affect the action of what you are doing, which in turn leads to hoping you don't miss. The body follows what the mind is thinking, and you start to miss the target. Once this feeling of fear sets in and you can feel it in your stomach, then the confidence goes and so does the throw.

Maybe you then begin to think about what part of the throwing procedure is out of sync. All of a sudden, you have changed your focus from the target to the throw, and then nothing feels right. If your thought process is out of sync with the muscle memory, the mind will try to make corrections which is what is throwing things out of sync. You might think it is the object you are throwing that is the issue, and pretty soon, you just feel nervous.

The only problem here is, you are no longer in your comfort zone. Your mind with the nonphysical thought is not in sync with the muscle memory of the physical body. This is usually the point when one might drink an alcoholic beverage or resort to some kind of superstitious action. These things simply calm the sense of fear and your focus is adjusted back to where it needs to be. Pretty soon, the drink or action, which appears to help the focus, becomes a requirement for the action to succeed. So, you think.

Practicing something over and over to the point the thought turns into action is a reflex. The mind and body act in one smooth motion. I believe this is because the life energy of both the mind and body is vibrating at the same frequency. When this happens, there is no need to self-judge or even really concentrate or focus on the action or the transfer of nonphysical thought energy to a physical action; it just happens as expected.

Happiness is when your "happenings are happening the way you want them to happen." When you are happy and carefree, the mind and body are just vibrating or humming at the same speed. There is no conflict at all, so the "think and do" process simply turns into an effortless *do*. Without self-awareness of how our minds work, we forget the mind controls the thought that, in turn, controls the body.

After the body has muscle memory, it no longer requires an actual thought for movement or action—you just walk, talk, or do. However, if you are not providing good food and water for energy to your physical body, everything you try to do becomes a struggle. Our bodies also require proper sleep and rest. There is a rare disease called perception where the ability to move doesn't exist because the feedback from the muscles stops. So, in order to move, you have to make visual contact with the part of the body you are trying to move and focus your thought energy directly to the part you want to move. If you can't see it, it doesn't move.

You see, when we begin to doubt or not trust ourselves, the fear energy comes alive and changes the unconscious flow or the way we focus our thought energy into action. For example, let us use the action of walking. If you are on the sidewalk and come across a two-inch-wide strip painted in a nice, straight line in front of you, it is easy to put one foot in front of the other, right on top of the line. If you turn that sidewalk into a wall, the ease is challenged. Even if the wall is a full twelve inches wide, if it is ten feet tall, there is a chance of falling off. Then the self-preserving emotion of fear is triggered, and the thought process changes.

Pretty soon, you think, *What if I fall off?* The fear makes you not trust yourself to the point you might just sit down because even though you are a very good walker, the mind is not comfortable with letting the thought process control the action. Even in the case where an injury prevents a connection between our brain and movement of our limbs, we can learn other ways to get through life. We can even learn to move prosthetics physically wired to the brain.

The mind knows our thought uses knowledge made up of different beliefs. So, if the belief of falling carries more power than the belief of not falling, the mind will let us know by stimulating a sense of fear. This sense of fear is there to help us focus more energy on the belief of knowing how not to fall. It is up to oneself to focus thought energy on the correct belief. Therefore, if the wrong thought creates a confused action, we can fall and get hurt.

So, with practice, we learn to not let the energy fear creates interfere with the thought that turns into action. Any habit we have—whether smoking, drinking, drugs, or superstitions—that comforts the mind by helping control fear becomes a need, so we think. Any thought that helps the mind and body vibrate at the same frequency may become a necessary thought.

With self-awareness and practice, we can change any fear-based thought. It is really only a matter of not giving a thought of fear any energy to thrive on. When the body and the mind work or vibrate as one, then the control of thought and knowledge is easier. If you can come to the understanding that any mind-altering substance only confuses this mind-body relationship, then with practice, you can create or stop any habit. Why not practice habits which make life easier?

If what we practice in life is in support of the good of the universe and supports life, the universe will give us the energy to complete the practice. Practice makes perfect, as long as the correct procedure is applied. Speed comes with accuracy, and accuracy comes from focusing with all your being. If you don't like what you are doing, you won't focus with your whole being and the task at hand will appear to take much longer.

If you love what you are doing, you will find the money thing to somewhat take care of itself. Our capitalist attitudes of making money off someone else's labor, in my mind, is still a form of slavery. The fact that if someone pays you what you're worth, they wouldn't make any money is bad practice in my eyes. In time, the dog-eat-dog corporate attitude, where CEOs get paid hundreds of millions of dollars off the backs of impoverished workers, isn't self-sustainable.

We are all the same us humans. We all function, with the same brain and internal organs; and if no one had skin, it would be impossible to tell us apart. The imbalance in levels of wealth in the world, in time, will come to a tipping point; and there won't be a wall or fence tall enough to stop the impoverished masses from overtaking those who try to hide behind their wealth.

Bad, unsustainable practices will always right themselves in time. However, the time line is always longer than an individual's life span. So, we all need to focus our practices in our own little worlds, with love for each other, as to help each other achieve reasonable comforts and securities in life with thoughts of practices, which help all involved. The universe will love those with unselfish practices.

Chapter 12

What's Love Got to Do with It?

"Why don't you love me anymore?" is a sentence we often hear. Do you have a definition of *love*? Why not? How can you understand anything you haven't defined?

I find my thought process is easier to control if I define the knowledge it uses. Are you controlling knowledge, or is knowledge controlling you? The simplest way to define *love*, to me, is with the example of vibration and frequency. I think when the mind and the body are vibrating in unison or on the same frequency and the thought process is not "inter*fear*ing," then this harmony creates the sense of love.

When we are just effortlessly enjoying life, we find it easy to harmonize our frequency to anything else's frequency. This includes animals as well as people. Even plants grow healthier with loving attention and the frequency of soothing music.

I believe since all of life energy is vibrating at different frequencies, in order to make a true connection, we focus our energy on looking at something; and if that vibrating energy is in tune with our frequency, then a feeling of love is sensed. As long as two people are of similar frequencies, the law of attraction takes to bringing them together. The closer the vibrating frequency, the stronger the love. Once you become aware that you are in control of your vibration, you can choose to vibrate at different levels. Therefore, love is a choice. Or is it?

The word *love* stimulates a lot of confusing feelings. Perhaps we should focus on what love is not. Is love just an idea we feel we must do in order to enjoy life? Isn't to love life simply to accept all the positive and the negative as they are for what they are?

Love isn't something you give and then take away. Love has nothing to do with honor or condition. Love is not the opposite of hate, no more than humility is the opposite of vanity. To kill for the love of your country isn't love. Love has nothing to do with obedience.

Sex without love is just sex. It is part of nature's way of guaranteeing the survival of the species. The fear of losing something that brings you pleasure, which causes the pain of jealousy, is from desire more than love. If you truly love someone, you don't want to hurt the relationship by causing jealousy. If someone is cheating on someone else to be with you, then they will have no problem cheating on you.

If someone is insecure, then they have problems loving themselves, so they will find it hard to believe anyone else will love them. If you don't know who or what you want to be, you can't be good for anyone else. One needs to be single for at least one year after a relationship to heal before starting another. If you feel you want to change someone, then you do not love them for who they are. If they feel you need to change, then they cannot love you for who you are. Why not find someone you don't feel the need to change? That is much easier than trying to change yourself or someone else.

Though these are basic guidelines for me to reflect on for myself to decide on the degree of love I have for a person, they may help you on opening your mind to *why* you love or just like someone.

The truth of the matter is, in order for you to know what love is and what love is for, you have to go deep inside yourself. You have to look at why you are suffering. You have to look at what you fear and why you fear it. Then you can learn to accept it for what it is. Then with the power of love, you come to forgive yourself. To see and accept your part in failed relationships is where forgiveness begins. To just look at what the other person, in a failed relationship, did to you will surely keep you suffering for a long time.

The forgiveness allows the suffering in the past to die. Then comes the resurrection of a new way of life and a new way of thinking. With this comes a whole new energy level. This energy vibrates at a much higher level than before. With this higher level of vibration comes the sense of beauty. This beauty is the same we see in the blossom of a flower or a sunset. We then radiate love like the blossom radiates its sweet smell for all who choose to smell it.

If all the things you create or make come from a place of love, those things will almost always be well received. For example, if the person who roasts the coffee you are drinking loves roasting coffee and is in a state of love when doing the roast, the positive energy it then possesses seems to make anyone who drinks it say, "Mmm, that's good coffee."

If you are in the state of not liking yourself, you will never stop to smell the roses. If you can't see the sweet smell of a flower as being love coming from the flower for all the world to enjoy, then you are probably vibrating at a low frequency. Perhaps you are just a negative person.

Maybe you haven't discovered your inner alliance, which consists of controlling what you think because of what you feel.

This intelligence is part of instinct. Perhaps you would rather allow your thinking or knowledge to dictate to you what to feel. Perhaps this is where the Bible story about the serpent in the tree of knowledge comes from. Listen to the serpent and knowledge controls you. Listen to your feelings and the energy you feel gives you the power to control both knowledge and the serpent.

If you see the energy as something you label as god, then this power of god allows you to control the serpent with knowledge. Do you think if the serpent—which we label as the devil—knows it can only use knowledge to control us, then why would the devil want us to know we can use our thought energy or god to control evil? It is one's choice to believe any of it. We even choose how we want to perceive the knowledge.

Let's just say the more positive you are, the faster the vibration. Therefore, the easier or more likely it is for your frequency to match other frequencies. The better you are at controlling your thought, the better you are at controlling your frequency, so the better you are at creating the sensation of love.

Whenever you find it easy to vibrate with all the world around, you are feeling love with everything, so your energy tank is full of energy to use to create anything you desire. This gives you a feeling of satisfaction. Isn't a life of satisfaction the thing we really crave? If you can get to the place where you love life, you will find life will love you back. It's almost a state of mind where nothing bad happens. Though misfortune and chaos is happening all around you, it's nothing but dust in the wind. It's like the little baby who is found completely unharmed in the basket on top of the pile of undistinguishable rubble that was a house just moments before the tornado came through.

If love is the vibrational harmony of the energy your mind and body are radiating, everything you get close to is influenced by you, just like you can let anything you get close to influence your vibration. If you come in contact with another person who is vibrating at a lower frequency or feeling down, through communication of some kind, you either choose to stay at your level of vibration or you can choose to let some of your energy go to them to increase their frequency. This usually makes them feel better; however, it can also lower your frequency. It is a drain from your fuel tank of energy to theirs. However, this life energy is plentiful because it radiates from everything. It is your choice in how much you waste on thought or fear or physical action.

If you stay aware on how you feel, then you know what level your tank is. It is your choice how high or low you keep your life energy tank. When you feel the sensation of love, you are adding energy to your tank. True love contains enough power to forgive almost anything. It's your choice how much power you give to anger. If you think you love someone who is abusing you and you continue to allow this abuse, you need to seriously question yourself as to why you think you love that person.

Often, we stay in abusive relationships because of the lack of love we have for ourselves. If you are self-abusive, you will often find you will tolerate the same amount of abuse from someone else as you are willing to take from yourself. For example, if you are abusing drugs and the pain and suffering you are inflicting on your body and soul isn't any worse than the pain and suffering someone else is causing you, it is likely you will stay in that relationship until the pain and suffering they inflict exceeds what you are willing to tolerate from yourself.

When sound is applied, everything in life resonates with frequency or vibration. Some things vibrate more than others with the same sound. When two people are vibrating at the same frequency, they both gain energy from this thing we call life. They choose to increase their frequency together and both feel the boost of energy. How can you not love that?

If you can come to the realization love is a choice, the fear of losing love would disappear. The fear of losing love comes from using thought energy on an assumption. Since thought energy requires physical energy to think, you are wasting energy on negative thought. Since love is the feeling that tells us we are gaining energy, then wasting energy on worry or fear naturally stops or confuses the sensation of love. If you nurture and love a plant, it grows and flourishes; and you feel love coming out of the healthy plant. You both gain the energy to satisfy life. When you are receiving love, you feel satisfaction.

Why not practice the things that create a life of love so you have energy for anything you want to create? Have you ever noticed when you get together or talk to certain people, both of your energy levels increase to the point you feel buzzed or energized? This happens even with people who are the same sex. If you get to work on a project together with one of these people, amazing things seem to happen and get done. Time just flies, and problems get solved without conflict. If the project is for the good of the people and the universe, the sense of accomplishment and satisfaction is no doubt best described as love.

If one can become aware that what we believe and put our faith in is not always true, then we learn to use our thoughts in ways to gain energy and/or the sense of love. Self-awareness is the allowing of feelings to guide our thought in the ways which gain the energy needed to live and solve the problems we face. When we focus our energy on protecting beliefs that give us a false sense of safety or security, then we will feel a lack of love. The sense of love comes from an action that creates personal energy, either physical or nonphysical. Everybody loves energy. If energy is God and God is energy, then, like it or not, even an atheist has energy or God. If energy creates a sense of love, then you can't help but love God.

Chapter 13

Why Am I Not Satisfied?

Satisfy. 1. to please someone by doing or giving them what they want or need. 2. to meet demands, wants, desires, or needs.

Now that I have touched on a lot of the things I believe to be important in the art of understanding what life is about, I would like to summarize a bit.

The game of life is full of ups and downs, good and bad, positive and negative. We eat and drink for the physical energy the physical body requires for life. The food we eat has also been alive in one form or another with the spark of life energy I refer to as God. When we eat food and drink that supports life in our bodies, we feel satisfaction or a feeling of being full. Please understand, though this appears to be me picking on overweight people, you can replace the word *food* with *drugs* or anything one might overindulge in.

An overweight person may feel empty because of the lack of love they have for themselves. Food fills the emptiness they feel inside and brings temporary fulfilment or satisfaction. Pretty soon, they hate themselves for the way they look. However, the only thing that makes them feel better is the feeling of fullness they receive from eating. The more you eat, the more you can eat, so the more it takes to feel full. Pretty soon, they just want to die, so they eat themselves to death.

Though there are certain diseases that can cause obesity, it is usually cured by stapling the stomach, making it smaller, which, in turn, creates a sensation of feeling full. A need for cheap processed food doesn't help, especially when stuff that is bad for you tastes so good. This is what leads to overweight poor people.

It is rarely a case of lazy people getting fat off the government. More often than not, it's due to the fact someone is making money off the unhealthy processed food they themselves don't eat. They are usually the first ones to bitch about the government regulation, which affects their bottom line.

We all need to become aware that we need to learn how to take care of ourselves, and what we feed ourselves is huge. Sometimes, health doesn't taste good, which means you have to learn what to like. Things like alcohol and other foods one may dislike can, in time, become an acquired taste.

All animals also survive or live through the same process of eating and drinking. In order to reproduce and find food and water—all the basics of life—we use a brain that thinks and remembers. This thought energy resides in the nonphysical dimension, which uses words or language of one form or another to communicate with oneself and/or others.

To keep order in life, life requires some laws that are not negotiable. I call these the laws of nature. These laws govern the whole universe. Without these laws, life would cease to exist. These laws of nature govern all the power or energy and the flow of energy in all dimensions of life. I call it God's law. However, you may call it Mother Nature. It doesn't matter what you label it. It's just what it has to be. Some call it the food chain. Everything that lives, dies and becomes food for more living things.

If the manufacturing world would use the rule of any by-product resulting from making something needs to be biodegradable or food for bacteria of some kind, we would have much less hazardous waste, which is unsustainable. Anything that doesn't go away—like plastic, for example—in time, will clog the food chain, which, in time, kills the natural process of being digested. Animal waste is fertilizer for dirt to nourish plants, which scrubs our air from CO_2 and releases oxygen, which all living beings need to breathe. Not to mention plants are also food for animals, which become food for humans. This process is what satisfies the energy need all life requires.

Please allow me to reiterate. To keep the dimensional thing in perspective, I like to look at a physical dimension and a nonphysical dimension. The physical dimension is the one we can see with our physical eyes and feel with our physical touch. The nonphysical dimension is the one we see with the mind's eye and feel with emotion.

All thought is made up of nonphysical energy in the form of words or language, which translate to knowledge, which is made up of everything we have ever learned—all our languages and beliefs, true and false. Intelligence or intuition is the way we develop our truths in order to control knowledge and our beliefs to enjoy life in the now. This also includes the natural instincts and/or laws of nature.

The art of learning what is true in our knowledge with our intelligence is wisdom. With wisdom, one uses the nonphysical energy of thought to live and survive by converting the nonphysical energy into physical energy. An intelligent being uses intent to convert the physical energy into positive actions, which lead to a life of enjoyment and fulfilment. An intelligent person is wise enough to not interfere or judge others who are learning about life. This leads to a life free from judgment and the negative thought which brings bad feelings or fear.

When we become self-aware of why we believe something, we can put ourselves in someone else's position to gain insight on where their perspective might be. The best way to understand where someone is coming from is to "walk a mile in their shoes," as they say. Meaning, the best way to relate to someone is to have personal experiences, which compare to their experiences, which help you understand what they might be feeling and *why*.

The reason *why* this is important in achieving a sense of satisfaction is, because everything we do in life is in relation to what we want and expect out of life. Anything we get or don't get is because of the way we relate with people, God, our surroundings, the law, and, most of all, ourselves. Everything that moves or flows—people, energy, a river, the wind, rain, the expansion of the universe, the movement of continents—is always in relation to something else. Every action has a reaction. If one can relate with all that is life through the relationship one has with themselves in their own life, satisfaction is guaranteed.

"A wise man learns from his own mistakes—a genius learns from someone else's," the adage says. To understand your own fears is how one can help another with their fears, which is satisfying to both parties. The definition of insanity is doing the same action over and over expecting a different result, as the saying goes. If you can use the knowledge you have to help others to help you, then everyone gains and satisfaction is the result.

If the relationship you have with yourself isn't based on truth that's provable through science and physics, along with understanding *why* you feel what you feel and think what you think, you may struggle with how to relate with the world. You won't be satisfied with guesses and assumptions. To know what the truth is, is much more acceptable than to believe you do, with nothing but thoughts and legends to back it up.

The best way to relate with people is to think *of* them first and listen to what they want or expect, and then you will know if helping them will help you, which is a win-win. To listen to others is how one learns what to expect. Satisfaction comes from everybody's expectations being met. If what you expect is undesirable or bad after it becomes reality, it is then satisfied so you can move on. For example, if you get fined for something that wasn't your fault, you pay the fine which, in turn, satisfies the judgment and you move on.

After a person knows what to expect, they then use judgment in the correct way, which allows the power of love to guide us to a life that is full of energy. We only need to judge how we feel as good or bad. With a life full of positive energy, there is no need for drugs or addictions to make one feel better. With this newfound freedom, one practices the things in life that create actions they love to do.

Though society labels actions as either good or bad, I like to look at it as that positive actions lead to life and negative actions lead to death. However, since death is a natural part of life that is very necessary to keep balance, then to each their own. We really do have a choice of life or death. The universe will only provide us with the energy that supports what we think. It doesn't care whether it is positive or negative. If you can realize the thought to just be positive or negative energy before you focus your energy on what it says, you can learn to let it go before you use personal physical energy in the form of emotion.

That is why we have the freedom to choose what we love to do to keep ourselves satisfied. It is up to us to become self-aware. It is our intention that determines what or how much we get. So be wise with your intelligence and allow your feelings to guide you to what you love or away from what you don't. Be careful with actions made out of confusion because they can only create more confusion. A life of confusion is anything but satisfying. If you don't make a point to figure out exactly *what* you want and *why* you want it, you will find everything in life confusing.

Does not a dog who chases his own tail catch it, when he wants to? Even though he would do better to chase food, sometimes acts of insanity are important to learn and confirm the direction one desires. Practice makes perfect. Positive or negative, both are needed. You can label it anything that works for you—just remember that action leads to positive results and inaction leads to the default, which is negative.

The more you act toward what you want, the more you get. You just have to keep focused in your thoughts and actions on what you want, and then the question of why you want it will become clear. When you know why, you can focus on the how to get what you want. Of course, what you want needs to be good for you. One also needs to realize what or how much one really needs to be satisfied.

Remember, the universe looks at what you think as being everything you want, so the law is, you attract what you think. You truly get what you believe you can. If a belief makes you feel funny, it probably is funny, so choose your beliefs wisely and know the truth is alive and changing. Live the truth that is only alive in this moment and right in front of you, and you and only you can produce this life of satisfaction guaranteed.

The only guarantees in life are the ones you create. All is fair in love and war, so it is fair to say some will love war. These people understand the sense of fear that leads to fight or flight, so they pick out the ones who are willing to fight. Not all people have good intentions, so be aware of why someone wants to help you.

If you can learn that confusion comes from fear, then you can practice not giving your energy to fear. Actions that come from confusion can only create confusion. When you find yourself lost in confusion, stop and ask yourself questions until the confusion is gone. If you can learn to let the past die, then you no longer waste your energy on it. Therefore, you have all the energy needed to live and love in the present. Then you are free to create a life of satisfaction the intelligence of knowing natural law brings.

All the things we practice in life lead to what we think we know life to be. All the things in life that we learn that become the knowledge which thought turns into beliefs a lot of the time are not necessarily true. Once we agree to a belief, we give the belief faith. As soon as we put faith in something, belief makes us feel safe. When we feel safe, anything that challenges or confuses the feeling of safety triggers the sense of fear. Anytime we have the feeling of fear, the body uses up a lot of physical energy. Fear in the mind allows the flow of thought energy to physical energy for self-preservation.

Have you ever noticed when you are doing something you love to do how it doesn't seem to take any energy and how time flies? Have you never asked yourself why that is? If so, what was your answer? Perhaps, it just didn't matter because you were just living in the moment enjoying the action.

If and when you learn to live in the moment without all the negativity of the past or what might happen in the future, it becomes easy to do things with the sense of love as a guide. This, as does everything in life, requires practice. So why not practice things that support and prolong a healthy life?

Perhaps you are saying to yourself, "I love doing drugs because they make me feel good." Yes, this is true, but only in the moment. This is one of the reasons why I say the truth is always alive and changing. This is also proof why living in the moment without thinking of the past or the future is also very satisfying. However, the mistake you are making from doing drugs comes from desire, not love. Just because it makes you feel better doesn't make it good for you. Learn to desire things that are truly good for you. Self-love will then be automatic.

It is very true that desire is an important tool in finding things that are going to create the sense of love. The true sense of love only comes from actions that fulfill a need which supports all life in the positive form. If you don't separate desire from love by asking why you desire, the results can be mistaken for love.

Desire has pain for a shadow, and love knows no pain. I know the reason I desired drugs was to take my mind off the thoughts that caused mental or physical pain. Desire, without the knowledge of what love is and what love is for, will always have pain as a companion. If the reason one does something they desire is because they are seeking comfort from something else, then they need to look at what or why they are uncomfortable. If you find yourself in a position of addiction, why not take advantage of one of the many free groups that are everywhere?

Most of the time, we are uncomfortable because of things we are thinking about and we are not sure what to do. This raises a sense of fear, so we try to ignore it or run away from it. The desire to avoid anything only produces the power to create it. Since this power comes from you anyway, why not focus the power on a solution to the problem? Since the knowledge we use to think is how we determine what to do, then going and listening to a group of people who have experienced or are experiencing the things you are trying to figure out works well.

The more knowledge you have about a problem you are trying to solve, the easier it is to find a solution. Most cures are learned from a group focusing on solutions. With practice, you can learn to focus you energy on solutions to your problems. With the sensation of love for yourself as a guide, the correct solution will become evident.

The easiest way can be the hardest to learn. There is a lot of satisfaction in solving our problems. You will find it easy to love yourself for at least trying to solve your own problems. The fact of the matter is, you are truly the only one who can solve your problems. If you are constantly looking to someone else for answers, then you will have a mind full of what works for them. Though this information or knowledge can assist you in finding the answers that fulfill your needs, only you can determine your truth.

Going to group therapy is a wonderful place to acquire tools to help yourself recover from addiction. There is not a human alive that wouldn't benefit from doing a twelve-step program. In fact, it should probably be part of the high school curriculum. Addiction is a disease that all humans have. Just like the common cold, everyone gets one sooner or later.

Though I stress on taking care of oneself as being key to personal freedom, life by design requires interaction with others. We are supposed to help each other, not conflict with each other. We are supposed to learn from each other, not necessarily teach what we believe to be true. Everyone is a teacher as well as a student. However, the only person we need authority over is ourselves.

To try and protect someone from themselves is only futile most of the time. We have no right to tell someone else they are screwing up when we are in a constant state of learning how not to screw up ourselves. We can pass along knowledge we have acquired about any situation to others, and the power of the word is very powerful.

When a person comes to understand the magic words and language have, they learn that the intent they use to project this magic is what creates a positive or negative outcome. If one can keep their personal judge to just judging what feels good or bad to oneself, then you will find that other people are more willing to listen. It's good to remember that no one wants to get yelled at.

How do you respond when someone yells at you? I know, with me, my reaction is always defensive at first. However, I have learned that if I step back out of their swinging range and hear them out, then I can use intelligence to decide what to do.

All yelling is a result of fear-based thought. It is also a good thing if someone who is attempting to abuse you walks away. There is a lot of abuse in the world today. If, at the first sign of abuse, you don't walk away from the abuser, then you might be letting yourself get sucked into a long period of abuse.

It always starts small with a little verbal abuse. If you feel a need to tolerate that, there is something wrong. We will tolerate the same amount of abuse from someone else that we are willing to inflict on ourselves. So, if we are very self-abusive, then we will allow others to abuse us as well.

This is why it is so important for us to become self-aware. We need to become aware that we are constantly talking to ourselves. We need to become aware that we are constantly judging everything and anything all the time—everything!

We need to become aware that we are in a relationship with everything around us in life. When we pay attention to how the mind works, using thoughts that are constantly comparing and complaining to itself about ourselves, then this interrelationship becomes self-awareness. With this self-awareness, you build your interalliance, which is intelligence. Then you can relate to anything or anyone you choose to. Then you begin to use forethought to see and avoid conflict before it happens.

With this foresight comes happiness and energy. Those of us who were abused by adults when we were children need to realize that it wasn't our fault. Though it wasn't our fault, we are still responsible for acknowledging how wrong it was, as to not turn it into something we need to avenge. We need to take a hard look at this before we can look at it and let it go. Forgiveness doesn't condone what they did; forgiveness is to free oneself from carrying the pain on through life. This is why it's important to let the past die.

You and only you have the power to create your world the way you want it. Only you know why you believe things. If you can look at and live life with the belief that you can create and will create, whatever you think about, then why not think or create a life where the amount of love you feel for yourself and all that is life is endless in the amount of energy required to maintain and create more of the same energy? What you think is *why* you do *what* you do; therefore, you have the choice of thinking about living in this moment, which is the perfect opportunity to start the life creation of your choosing. Or you can live life in the past, which is always old, just like the thought of death being void of new life and the fun of learning.

Learn to practice the actions or thoughts that lead to a life full of energy, which we can measure by the sensation of love, which tells us why we chose this life. If this life is the only one you get, why not enjoy all that you create that in turn creates the continuance of life? There is nothing more satisfying in life than the things we do that fulfill our needs to live life.

Life can be very satisfying when we choose to learn how to solve our own problems. If you choose to re*lie* on what others tell you, then you will surely experience a lot of confused mixed emotions. Why not use your feelings in the correct way?

If you can look at feelings as either bad or good, then all the different labels we give to our feelings won't be so confusing. You can learn to answer all your own questions of why you think and do what you do. Only you can answer these questions anyway. Then you will automatically learn what you want and need to do for yourself.

You can't help anyone else if you can't help yourself. If you are in the process of helping yourself, you will find the universe produces the right people and things to help you. Things that you need just show up. If you don't believe this can happen, then you won't see it when it does show up.

Self-love comes from self-help. If it weren't for self-inflicted wounds, we would have no problems. Self-satisfaction can only come from actions that create a sense of self-love. Without self-love, you can't know how to use all the love the universe is always providing you.

Self-judgment stops self-love, only if you don't choose to ask yourself why you are judging. The best way to satisfy any judge is with a true answer of *why*. Once you know and accept the truth of *why*, then you can choose to move on to the fact that what is done is done and only you have the power to let it go.

If you know *why*, then you can learn *how*. Sometimes you may never find out why, so why not try to just move on? Some answers just take time. Sometimes, you need more information. The best way to acquire information is to ask questions. You always have the right to ask questions. Everyone also has the right to say no. A mind that is not worrying about the past is open to the answers that are coming forth that will explain the past. Sometimes, where answers come from doesn't necessarily need to make sense. Sometimes, the answers come from people I don't exactly care for. Even fictional stories can contain some truth. However, I rarely hear what I need to if I am delving in the past.

The best thing about the past is that it is done. It is your choice where you focus your power. If you choose to give the past power, then that power continues to give life to the past in the present. If you waste all your power on the past, there is no power for the present, which means no future. You have free will to let the past die, so you can create the new life of the future by being alive with new ideas that only live in the present. What doesn't kill you only makes you stronger. Thoughtless actions are usually the actions that kill you. You are only selfish if that action you are doing for yourself hurts someone else.

If you learn to ask yourself *why* before you act, then you naturally think before you act. If the answer you are coming up with for yourself doesn't trigger a sense of love, then you need to rethink the action. Remember, love is the gauge for gaining life energy. Fear requires energy for self-preservation. The stronger the fear, the more energy you use. Therefore, if your fear comes from thinking something might happen, then you are wasting precious energy you will need to survive, if it does happen. It is like living life with the attitude that there are no problems in life, only solutions. If you focus your life energy on solutions or actions of love for life, then all fear goes away.

If you are afraid to live life, then don't worry about it because you won't live very long. However, as soon as worry leaves the mind and the thought process, then you naturally look at the now and begin again to feel the flow of life energy through your entire being—from everything and everyone that loves you. The reason to why ask *why* is that if you don't, then you are leaving yourself open to the forces of the universe that use both positive and negative to create and maintain the flow of life energy. You and only you know why you do or want certain things.

As soon as you answer your own questions, you then know why you can use the power of the universe to create whatever you desire, bad or good. Things that feel bad lead to death, and things that feel good lead to the continuance of life. Death only makes room for new life. The reason why this has to be makes sense to me. To me, death is just the new beginning in a nonphysical dimension. If you know that life is eternal, would you take the time to perfect this life?

I like to look at the whole death thing as just a new beginning. Why? Because it makes me feel better. If I let all those thoughts of why I *can't*, die; then it is easy to let the thoughts of why I *can*, live. I also limit the judge in my mind to only judging my feelings of being either bad or good. Why? Because I can.

I have found that one can't be a good judge of any situation because one never gets the whole truth. Why? Because the truth is alive and always changing. The only real truth one can count on is their own truth. Even your own truth is alive and changing, so why put faith in the word *truth* at all? I find that if I only let the judge only judge the truth of what I am feeling, then life is less confusing. I also limit their rulings to either good feelings or bad feelings. Why? Because that is the only authority the judge needs to help me in life.

I also don't like to label situations as good or bad because the judge tends to think it needs to rule on all situations. Why? Because the judge wants to feel safe. Safe, to me, is just another feeling that falls under the label of good. If I look at situations as a reason *why* ask why I am in a particular situation, then I have the power to feel my way out of an undesirable situation or feel my way into desirable ones.

Better yet are actions done with the sense of love in mind rather than desire to avoid situations of pain, since actions of desire without love most always are accompanied by feelings of pain. Why this is and has to be is obvious to me. You will be best to come to your own conclusions on all of this information. As long as you do the best you can to understand and love yourself, in time, you will become self-aware and wise.

The best way to stop pain, especially mental pain, is through the love we have for one another using the art of forgiveness.

When one learns to cut out the thoughts that lead to suffering, then the thoughts of happiness and success can live on. With practice, one learns to choose thought wisely with the sense of love as a guide. A satisfying life that is full of energy can be the only result. Why or why not requires one to look at all the little pieces of life that one has to use to build life. Feed what you want to live and let die what you don't want in your life. There is no need to kill anything because everything dies eventually. It is the law of nature—waste not, want not.

To me, hope is another power that helps stop suffering. For most, God is an answer that creates hope for living. Perhaps God is hope. Or is God just the energy that hope creates? I sure hope you find the power that God is because the energy that comes with believing has the power to create all there is and all that can be.

Why not? It sure explains to me the why and how God is the Great Creator. God is the life energy that stimulates evolution to me. You either choose to evolve or dissolve. It's your free will—use it or lose it.

Chapter 14

Why Forgiveness?

Forgive them Father, for they know not what they do. (Luke 23:34, KJV)

Do you struggle with the reason why we need to forgive? I don't believe any human has ever not struggled with forgiveness. In your mind, who is forgiveness for? Is it for the person who hurt or let you down?

This is another topic religion is passionate about. Seems to me Jesus died because of our sins. If he died to free us from sin, then why is there still so much sinning? I'm sorry if this angers you; however, how do you know for sure things haven't got misunderstood in translation? What if Jesus said "Forgive them, Father, they know not what they do" because in his own mind, he had already forgiven those who were killing him as to free his own mind of the pain he didn't deserve? It's not like he didn't know he was going to be resurrected in the days to come. If he knew he was dying, he had to know he was coming back.

Was not Jesus supposed to be the living example of a way to live life? Was he not made up of the same flesh and blood us humans of the day are made of? I wasn't there, but I do know how bad human beings are at eye-witnessing; and things that appear miraculous tend to get exaggerated. Put passion on top of it, and it would have a hard time standing up in the court of law today.

Forgive me, but if Jesus showed up today, we as a society would probably do the same thing to him.

I believe forgiveness is for oneself to allow the pain and anguish one feels after someone else has wronged or hurt you to die so you can give them another chance, if they so deserve—a resurrection, if you will.

To forgive someone does not condone their actions; however, it requires one to put themselves in the wrongdoers' shoes as to gain an understanding to *why* they did what they did. If you can come to an understanding of the reason as to why they did what they did, you are well on your way to forgiveness. By no means this has to agree with what you believe or makes their actions right.

With that said, we will move on to the hardest person to forgive. I hope this far along in the book, you are looking at yourself. You might want to believe you have forgiven yourself; however, chances are, you have something you crucify yourself for on a regular basis. I know I do, but they are just little things which come and go in life on a daily basis. Mostly just those little mistakes that happen because I fail to focus both my mind's eye and my physical eyes on tasks at hand.

One of my new little sayings goes, "If one fixes the mistake before anyone else knows about it, can it even be considered a mistake at all?" Similar to the saying "If no one knows about it, it never even happened." Instant self-forgiveness.

Some mistakes take longer, but as long as they're in progress, I keep moving forward. Forgiveness is a daily, ongoing process one needs to practice daily, kind of like love. It is how we gain the energy needed to protect ourselves from those who know not what they do.

If you are looking to find who God is, you will tend to miss out on *what* God is. When you learn what God is, then the only who you need to trust in is you. God is the life energy that makes everything live. It is up to you how you use the energy that God is.

Is it not you who chooses whether a belief you are experiencing comes from the good that God is? Ever notice the first words out of the mouth of even a nonbeliever experiencing great fear or great pleasure usually has an "Oh god" somewhere in the statement? If you don't know who or what you are, you can't know who or what God is. Good luck on your journey to discovering why you are who you are.

Chapter 15

Moving from *Why* to *How*

Well, here we are in the beginning of the last chapter. So far, I hope I have shown you a reason to question all your thoughts and beliefs, especially when they are such a large part of everyday trials and tribulations. To become self-aware is how we decide on what life path may lead us to a more interesting and fulfilling way of life.

In the first chapter, my intention was to stimulate thoughts on how incredible the whole miraculous system we call life truly is. We as a human species have many more questions than answers when it comes to truly knowing why we are here, more so with where we are going.

Our planet is a mere speck in a universe so massive, only a few of us can even begin to fathom the size of it all. Though science learns more every day, most of the religions in the world are stuck in beliefs and legends of some two thousand years ago. We have come a long way; however, we still haven't figured out how to get along within ourselves, even with one another.

It seems to me we are the only living things on this planet that doesn't know why we are here and what purpose we are supposed to play. I am afraid I've lost my faith in religion due to the fact they have got it wrong so many times. This doesn't necessarily mean that all religions are wrong.

In my life experience, I have seen and found a little truth in all stories, be it fact or fiction. Though I have lost faith in religion, I still have faith in a higher power or a source of energy, which mixes and flows in and through all living things we know of and are discovering every day. We discover new life every day, on this one small planet—this one small planet in a universe of trillions of possibilities. I find if I use the word *god* to refer to all the miraculous things that this life contains, then my interactions with the God-fearing people who find comfort in religion is much more productive and enjoyable.

Science, to me, is also constantly learning and changing their minds on things; however, physical scientific facts explain and answer so many more of the *why* questions, and they update their history books as they learn the truth of things. Why the historians and religions don't change their beliefs to keep up with the facts science proves have plenty of explanations. I won't go into anymore in this book. I would rather look at how to better use my energy on helping my fellow man find his own answers to *why*. Life can be easier when you learn how to get along with yourself as well as others. It all has to do with the laws of relativity and relationships.

It is all about the energy and the way it flows because of the positive and negative, just like positive and negative thoughts only exist because you can't have one without the other. Thoughts are nonphysical because you can't see them with science; and they are energy because they trigger the brain, which in turn moves the physical body in which we—as a spiritual being in a physical body—create or destroy our personal world by the choices we make.

Since everything in existence is in relation to its surroundings, every action has a reaction. If it is in a physical dimension, it's affected by time and space; if it's in a nonphysical dimension, it's only limited to the size of the universe. It's how you control your actions that determines how the universe reacts to you. If you don't like your actions, I'm pretty sure you won't like the universe's reactions.

Since the thoughts you think come from the knowledge you believe and learn from the past, they better contain the truths of today, along with uncontaminated feelings and beliefs that are scientifically backed. This translates to the wisdom one needs to use the power of the words to judge the fear one has in life in order to practice the healthy addictions. And these healthy addictions lead to a life full of love, satisfaction, and forgiveness. That pretty much sums up what I am trying to achieve in this book.

The path to personal freedom only starts in the your own mind, after you decide you have suffered enough and want to experience more joy and love in this life. The age of this person can vary from young to old. Sadly, some don't come to this realization until they are on their deathbeds.

Many look to religion for the answers of divinity and find enough information to satisfy their questions why a need for a higher power termed *god* is important. It seems so obvious that we, as human beings, require rules and regulations and a constant reminder which tells us we need to treat each other better.

—Mark "the Spirit Welder" Murray

About the Author

Mark A. Murray, better known as Mark the Welder, was born in the Black Hills of South Dakota and now resides in the Rocky Mountains of Colorado. Mark is your typical, average man in size, looks, and background. However, Mark's life has been anything but typical.

Mark has pretty much marched to the beat of his own drum. This led to much conflict and plenty of time in trouble, as we say. Not so much a hardened criminal for things like robbery or battery, however, when it comes down to drugs and obeying authority, there were many problems. If not for his high school's welding program, Mark probably would not have finished high school. Mark was very lucky in finding his God-given talent in welding.

He excelled in the welding program so well, he finished the two-year program in the first year, was a student teacher throughout his senior year, and became a substitute teacher in the following years. He won the regional and state competitions in welding but was not allowed to compete at the national level due to a mix-up at the school with dues that did not get paid. As it turned out, his welding instructor paid his dues in the first quarter of his junior year, even though you cannot even compete until you are a senior.

The confidence the instructor felt was not shared by the head of student services at the time, so he put the dues in a welding file instead of the appropriate file where it was forgotten. Therefore, missing paying the dues on the deadline kept Mark from competing at the national level where he more than likely would have won. Internationals were held in Sydney, Australia, that year, so Mark felt pretty cheated in life.

This led to a life of much self-medication, failed relationships, and anger toward the structure of institutional society. This led to drug and alcohol arrests, which lead to government programs and psychological evaluations. However, the natural welding talent that pulled Mark through high school also pulled him through life, due to the fact it gave him the means to pay bills, fines, and those expenses life require.

Every person alive has a talent or something that comes easy to them, and to realize this early in life is a true blessing. All the problems that led to psychological programs, psychiatrists, and counselors are a blessing in disguise because Mark made it a point to learn all he could from them while he was there. So, by default, he became educated on and in the psychological world that he was exposed to.

Though it took forty-plus years of drug abuse and bad decisions that Mark made in his life experience, he now is very much a recovered addict. He now has good judgment without a need to judge others. Good judgment comes from experience, and experience comes from bad judgment.

Though many mistake God-given talent for their life purpose, Mark believes we all have the same life purpose—help each other by sharing the answer *why* we think we made the mistakes we have made. There is a true burst of energy one feels when they help others that makes life worth living. What this energy is and where it comes from is something that Mark has figured out and wishes to share this with the world by writing books for all to read.

This life energy requires much thought and is hard to explain because all we have been taught in life has led to false beliefs. Though Mark is intelligent and rather wise about life, he lacks a college education, which teaches big words and structure. His works will be less difficult for those who lack an education to read and understand, even those with a higher education should find Mark's works thought provoking.

Mark is writing the first in a series of books he terms *Why* books. Mark is now coming to the age in life where the physical demand of helping others with his welding skills will no longer be possible, so the next step is "Mark the Spirit Welder." Mark can only hope that his success as an author is a fraction of what his welding has been.

About the Book

A Reason Why to Ask Why basically derives from my life experiences where I have struggled. Things like the *god* concept, relationships, addiction, and things that caused me to suffer in life always had me asking the question of *Why do I do these things that cause me to suffer?* After many years of counseling, group therapy, Bible studies, and a whole lot of reading, I have finally come up with some answers.

Since I know that a lot of people struggle with the same things, I figured that maybe I could help others to realize that life can be a wonderful journey—when one understands why many of us suffer for no good reason. Most of it comes from the way we fall victim to our own thought patterns and the way we think about things.

So this is the first book in the series to help you begin to open your mind and become self-aware of your own beliefs. I urge you to ask yourself, *Why do I think like I do?* and *Is my own thinking stopping me from a life of satisfaction?*

No matter how bad you think your life may be, there is a brighter future in store for anyone who learns the reason for why to ask *why*.